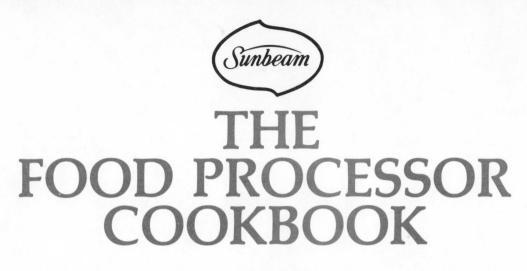

THE
FOOD PROCESSOR
COOKBOOK

New Ideas for Easy and Elegant Food Preparation · 250 Tested Recipes

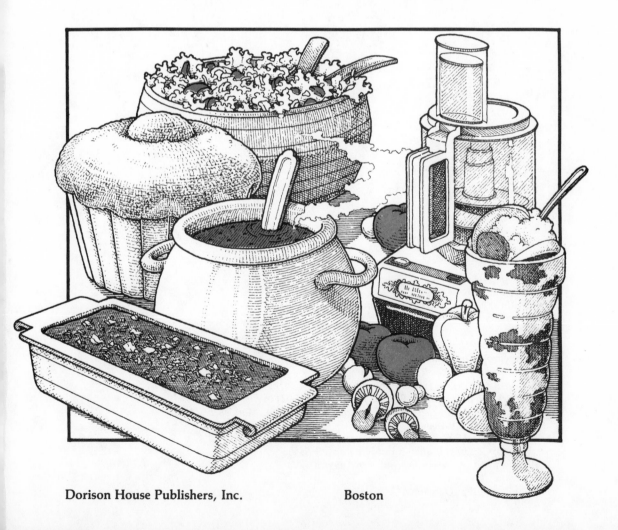

Dorison House Publishers, Inc.   **Boston**

®*SUNBEAM* ™*Le Chef*
©*Sunbeam Corporation, 1979*

Published by Dorison House Publishers, Inc.
824 Park Square Building, Boston, Massachusetts 02116
Cover design: Robert J. Benson, Cachalot Design Group, Marblehead, Mass.
Illustrations: Brian Cody
ISBN: 916752-35-6
Library of Congress Catalog Card Number: 79-65556
Manufactured in the United States of America

Second Printing December, 1980

THE CONTENTS TABLE

IMPORTANT SAFEGUARDS

When using electrical appliances, basic safety precautions should always be followed, including the following:

1. Read all instructions before using appliance.

2. To protect against electrical hazards, do not immerse base, cord, or plug in water or other liquid.

3. Close supervision is necessary when any appliance is used by or near children.

4. Unplug from outlet when not in use, before putting on or taking off parts, and before cleaning.

5. Avoid contacting moving parts. Make sure the motor has completely stopped before disassembling. Never feed food by hand when slicing or shredding. Always use food pusher.

6. Do not operate any appliance with a damaged cord set or after the appliance has been dropped or damaged in any manner. Return appliance to the nearest authorized service facility for examination, repair, or electrical or mechanical adjustment.

7. The use of attachments not recommended by the appliance manufacturer may cause hazards.

8. Do not use outdoors.

9. Do not let cord hang over edge of table or counter, or touch hot surfaces.

10. Do not use appliance for other than intended use.

11. Keep hands, as well as spatulas and other utensils, away from moving blades or discs to prevent injury or damage to the food processor. A scraper may be used but only when the food processor is not running.

12. Blades are sharp. Handle carefully.

13. To avoid injury, never place blade on the base without first having put the mixing container properly in place.

14. Always operate the food processor with the cover in place.

15. Do not attempt to defeat the cover interlock mechanism.

SAVE THESE INSTRUCTIONS

THE PLEASURES OF COOKING
WITH A FOOD PROCESSOR

Home cooks everywhere are turning to their food processors daily for help in their kitchens. This new and radically different appliance has just the right combination of speed and power to make its remarkable results possible. It's a boon to people who want to save time and effort in everyday cooking and also be able to make those recipes that are tedious or practically impossible to prepare without a processor.

The food processor's popularity is well deserved. It comes along just as lifestyles are changing. More women are employed outside their homes than ever in history, and time and work savers are considered necessities. Dinner can't wait when they get home. Moreover, the kitchen is no longer solely the woman's domain. Men and women — young and old — are sharing household tasks and striving for efficiency and high quality in all they do. They are intelligent and open to new ideas to improve their lives.

The appearance of the processor on the scene also coincides with the swell of interest in cooking and trying new tastes. Many people are collecting new recipes, perfecting old family favorites and experimenting with specialties from all parts of the world. Gourmet cooking is a favored hobby, with clubs forming for experienced cooks as well as novices.

Along with this desire for gastronomical delights is increasing knowledge about good nutrition. There is an awareness of the relationship of diet to health, and the food processor makes it easy to control the contents and freshness of the food you prepare. The powerful steel cutting blade allows you to chop your own meat so that you know what seasonings and fat are in it. Food from the family table can be quickly puréed for babies or special diets. A variety of preservative-free breads can be kneaded; additive-free cake batters, cookie doughs, sauces, and dressings can be mixed in the container. The capacity, size, and shape of the food processing container permits greater quantities of food to be processed than in a blender. Fruits and vegetables can be sliced in literally seconds before serving vitamin-filled salads or steamed side dishes.

As food prices rise daily, we're all interested in economy. When you have a food processor it's easy to be a thrifty cook and still retain elegance while practicing the culinary arts. Not a piece of bread is wasted, as dry pieces are whirled into bread crumbs. Leftovers get turned into delicious combinations as vegetables and cooked chicken are chopped and combined with broth to make Chicken Vegetable Soup or added to a couple of ounces of Cheddar cheese to become Chicken Cheese Spread. Bottled dressings and sauces on grocery shelves are bypassed since the processor makes them rapidly and superlatively for less money.

Start your adventure in food processor cooking with an easy recipe such as Guacamole. Then you might move on to all or part of a meal. Here is an example of a menu you could choose from the kitchen-tested recipes in this book:

Vichyssoise

Chicken with Mushroom Sauce

Sally Lunn Bread

Broccoli Casserole

Creamy Lettuce Salad

Chocolate Chip Ice Cream Pie

You should be old friends by now, and needn't be intimidated by recipes such as Gnocchi Verdi or Paté Brisée.

With your processor in hand, you can reintroduce old standbys such as coleslaws, potato pancakes, or hashed browns without scraping your fingertips. You'll slice onions without tears. As you mince mushrooms in moments, grate orange rind and fresh Parmesan, shred coconut, chop parsley, purée tomatoes or peas, crumb bread and crackers, knead, blend, and julienne, you'll constantly marvel at the quick work the processor makes of such tasks.

To help you make the most of your food processor's possibilities, this book includes "how-to" directions and photographs to show you techniques for successful food processing. It contains charts and tables to guide you in determining what blade or disc to use; how to proceed; what the resulting appearance will be of the food you're processing; and the amount of food you will have after the food has been processed. It tells you how the factors such as size, shape, quantity, quality, moisture content, texture, temperature, and whether or not the food has been precooked, affect the way to proceed.

Even a miracle machine like the food processor has limitations, and you should recognize them. For example, it won't beat egg whites stiff or double the volume of whipping cream. You'll want to use your electric mixer for that. It can't grind whole wheat to flour. It won't mash potatoes — they get gummy. Although it will pulverize coffee beans, the resulting coffee may not be to your taste. It can chop ice but it's not recommended that you do so because the blade would be damaged after continuous use.

So, let your food processor do what it does best, and you will surely enjoy the pleasures of cooking with a food processor.

THE FOOD PROCESSOR

How It Operates

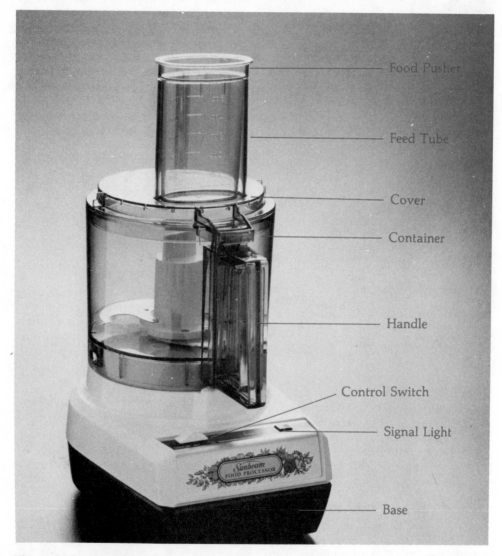

Food Pusher

Feed Tube

Cover

Container

Handle

Control Switch

Signal Light

Base

This is the Sunbeam Food Processor. It is a compact, simply-operated machine. Keep it on a dry, level countertop near your workspace, handy for frequent use.

The 7" x 9" electric power base houses a powerful, quiet motor — no belts to slip or break. It is protected against overheating and burn out by a built-in control device. When processing especially heavy mixtures for long periods of time, this protective device may "shut off" the motor to prevent overheating. If this should occur, turn the control switch to OFF and allow the motor to cool. This will avoid the unit turning ON unexpectedly. After a few minutes turn the unit ON again and complete your processing.

The **cover** must be locked in place before the food processor can be started. This also allows the cover to be used as an ON/OFF switch when the base switch is ON. Both the **cover** and **container** are made of durable, dishwasher-safe, see-through polycarbonate plastic with a large handle for easy pouring. A machine-powered spindle protrudes through the hole in the container on which the blade or disc is anchored. The container will hold up to 2½ cups of most foods. For larger amounts, divide in parts and process, emptying the ingredients into a bowl as the container fills. The cover has a **feed tube** through which ingredients are pushed onto the disc, or poured. The cover inverts to make the height of the unit only 12″—short enough to stand on a countertop underneath most kitchen wall cabinets.

The **food pusher** is used to press foods down the feed tube and keeps fingers free of moving parts. It can be used to measure ingredients, as it is graduated for U. S. and metric measurements up to 6 ounces, 180 milliliters.

The **control switch** on the left side of the base is pushed to the far right to turn the unit ON, or to the far left for a pulsing feature that allows you to snap it ON and OFF very quickly. This gives you better control during short processing times, and helps you to avoid overprocessing.

    To turn the motor OFF, slide the control switch to the center position. This will stop the motor. The "safety slowdown" feature reduces the speed of the blade or disc and helps it to come to a quick stop when the unit is turned off. **DO NOT REMOVE THE COVER OF THE UNIT UNTIL THE BLADE OR DISC COMES TO A COMPLETE STOP.**

The **signal light** on the right side of the base glows whenever the food processor is plugged in and ready for use.

The Food Processor is Versatile

It has several different attachments that allow you to get different results. Each blade and disc performs differently and yields a different textured food product. The recipes in this book tell you which blade or disc to use. You may also refer to the Food Processing Guide.

The **steel cutting blade** is the most valuable tool. It is used for chopping, blending, crumbing, grating, mincing, mixing, kneading, and puréeing foods... for preparing bread doughs, muffin batters, salad dressings, fillings, dips, and spreads. The nuts in the photograph were chopped by the **steel cutting blade**. Always use the easy-grip knob for quick and clean blade removal.

The **slicing disc** makes beautiful, uniform slices of raw fruits and vegetables, as shown in the photograph. It will also slice cooked vegetables, sausages, meats, and cheese. The thickness of the slices will depend somewhat on the amount of pressure put on the food pusher. More pressure gives thicker slices. Don't press too hard, however, because you could damage the disc.

The **shredding disc** shreds foods such as cheese, onions, potatoes, and other raw and cooked vegetables. You can control the length of the shreds by placing the vegetable into the feed tube vertically for short shreds (see those on the right) and horizontally for long shreds (see those on the left). Use finger holes to lift the shredding and slicing discs out of the container.

The **French fry cutter disc** (optional on some units) has a wider cutting space and cuts potatoes and soft vegetables such as eggplant and zucchini into even, uniform strips similar to French fries.

NOTE: Some units will be provided with a combination disc and separate drop-in slicer and shredder plates in lieu of separate slicing and shredding discs.

Using the Drop-in Plates

The **drop-in plates** are to be used with the **plate holder disc.**

Just drop the desired plate into the opening in the plate holder disc.

While processing, do **not** allow the container to become too full. Excess food may push the plate out of the disc and could damage the unit.

NOTE: Use extreme caution when handling the drop-in plates, as they are VERY SHARP!

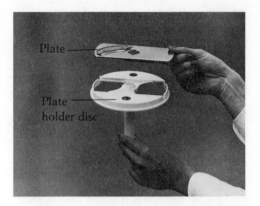

Attaching the Plate Holder Disc

Notice the flat guide inside the plate holder shaft. Position the disc so that the flat guide is directly above the flat side of the center shaft of the food processor.

Flat Guide on
Plate Holder Shaft

Use the finger holes provided to lower the disc to the bottom of the container.

After processing, use the finger holes provided to remove the plate holder disc.

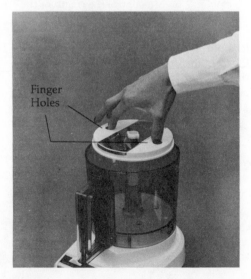

Then, gently push on the underside of the plate to remove it from its position in the disc.

In all of the recipes and instructions in the book, these are referred to as slicing disc and shredding disc.

The **plate holder disc** is used to hold the drop-in slicing or shredding plates.

The **shredding plate** is used with the plate holder disc for shredding vegetables and cheese.

The **slicing plate** is used with the plate holder disc for slicing fruits, vegetables, and meat; and for julienning carrots and potatoes.

PROCESSING POINTERS

Techniques For Successful Food Processing

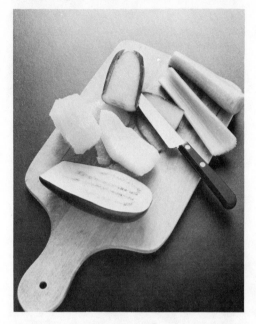

1. Trim Food to Fit the Feed Tube

Cut foods too large or round for the feed tube into pieces, or trim to fit. The eggplant has been cut in half lengthwise; the orange, peeled and trimmed; the cucumber, trimmed; a chunk of coconut cut to about 2" x 4"; long foods such as the carrot and celery stalk cut to about 5" lengths.

2. Don't Overload the Container

A large load results in unevenly chopped food. For example, chop 1 or 2 onions cut in halves or quarters (depending on the size) at a time. You will have evenly chopped onions, and they won't be overprocessed.

3. Use the Food Pusher to Press Foods Through the Feed Tube

Place food upright into the feed tube and use the food pusher to slice or shred. NEVER use your fingers to push the foods.

4. The Amount of Pressure You Put on the Food Depends on the Texture of the Food
Steady, even pressure is best for most foods. Use firm pressure on hard foods such as cucumber, potatoes, carrots, and celery; light pressure for delicate foods, such as strawberries and mushrooms. To slice potatoes thinly for potato chips, use light pressure.

5. For Larger Foods, Load From the Bottom of the Feed Tube
When food is too large to fit through the top of the feed tube, it may fit through the bottom opening which is a little larger.

6. The Best Temperature for Processing Depends on the Food
Uncooked meat should be trimmed, boned, and partially frozen on a cookie sheet until it is firm, but not solidly frozen. Thick pieces of meat should be cut to fit the feed tube. Thin, flat pieces, such as veal or chicken breasts, should be rolled up to insert from the bottom of the feed tube.

Cooked meat should be chilled. Remove fat and gristle and cube into 1″ pieces before chopping. Use TOUCH/ON control and chop coarsely for salads, or finely for spreads. For sliced meats, slice as you would sausages and luncheon meats—at refrigerator temperature.

Process fresh, crisp, firm vegetables and fruits at refrigerator temperature. Pack the feed tube with celery, as shown, alternating thick and thin ends, and slice with firm pressure.

Cheeses such as Cheddar, Swiss, and Muenster (soft cheeses) are best processed at refrigerator temperature. Process hard cheeses such as Parmesan and Romano at room temperature.

7. How Foods Are Cut Before Processing Affects Results

Cut long narrow foods such as the carrots shown in the photograph to about 5″ lengths and slice to produce round slices. Shreds will be short. Cut carrots into 2½″-pieces and arrange horizontally in the feed tube for long slices for Oriental dishes, or to scoop a cheese dip. Shreds will be long and attractive for salads.

Potatoes may be peeled, if desired, and halved or quartered to fit feed tube. With shredding disc in container, place potatoes in the feed tube, and press with food pusher. Place shredded potatoes in cold water until you are ready to fry them, to prevent darkening. Dry on paper towels before frying.

For whole slices, choose small potatoes to fit the feed tube. Cut larger potatoes in halves or quarters to fit the feed tube. Unpeeled potatoes are more nutritious and attractive when sliced. With slicing disc in place, press food pusher onto potatoes firmly.

8. Cut Foods into Uniform Pieces When Blending, Chopping, Mixing, and Puréeing

Prepare foods for processing by cutting them into as nearly uniform pieces as possible so that they are evenly chopped. When there are some large and some small pieces the large pieces are left coarse and the small ones are overprocessed.

9. Liquids May Be Added Through the Feed Tube

While processing other ingredients, liquids may be added through the feed tube. Use the food pusher, a measuring cup, or pitcher for easier pouring.

10. Single Foods are Placed on the Left Side of the Feed Tube

A single food, such as the carrot shown, is sliced by placing it on the left side of the feed tube. Hold it in place with the food pusher. The clockwise rotation of the disc pushes it against the side of the tube, helping it to stay upright.

11. When Slicing Small Foods, Layer the Food in the Feed Tube

To slice mushrooms or other light, small fruits or vegetables, such as the strawberries shown in the photograph, stack them sideways in the feed tube, placing them in alternating directions, densely packed. Slice with moderate pressure.

How To Perform Basic Functions

Chop

Place steel cutting blade into container. Place all ingredients into processing container. Process, using TOUCH/ON control, until desired consistency is reached. Meat can be made into paté in a few seconds. Be careful not to overprocess. Look away, and you can have liquified green pepper!

Suggested foods: apples, celery, mushrooms, carrots, cabbage, nuts, onions, parsley, raw meat, cooked meat (ham, chicken, beef, turkey, liver), seafood, hard-cooked eggs, corn chips, olives, pickles, pimiento, tomatoes.

Crumb

Place steel cutting blade into container.
Fine crumbs: While processor is running, drop pieces of food down feed tube. Process until you have the desired consistency.
Coarse crumbs: With steel cutting blade in place, put pieces of food into processing container. Process, using TOUCH/ON control until there are coarse crumbs.
Suggested foods: Crackers, cookies, dry or fresh bread.

Blend

Place steel cutting blade into container. Place all ingredients into container, and process until smooth.

Suggested foods: Dressings, sauces, dips, spreads, flavored butters, gelatins, milk shakes.

Julienne

Place slicing disc into container. Slice food. Pack sliced food lengthwise horizontally into the feed tube. Slice again.

Suggested foods: Carrots, potatoes.

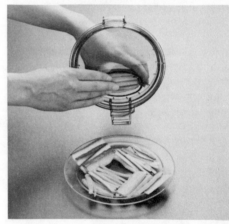

French Cut

Place slicing disc into container. Cut food in 2" to 2½" lengths; stack in feed tube horizontally, using spatula to hold them while arranging. Slice with light pressure.

Suggested food: Green beans.

Grate

Place steel cutting blade into container. Cut foods into 1" cubes. (Hard cheeses should be at room temperature.) Place all ingredients into container. Process, using TOUCH/ON control, until desired consistency.
Suggested foods: Hard cheeses such as Parmesan and Romano.

Knead

Place steel cutting blade into processing container. Put flour (not to exceed 3½ cups) and other ingredients into the container. Process, just until the dough ball is formed.
Suggested food: Bread dough.

Purée

Place steel cutting blade into processing container. Add ingredients. Process until smooth.
Suggested foods: Fresh, cooked, or canned fruits (such as peaches, bananas, apples, pears, strawberries), and fresh, cooked, or canned vegetables (such as carrots, beans, potatoes, corn, tomatoes, peas).

Mince

Place steel cutting blade into processing container. While food processor is running, drop food down feed tube. Food minces very quickly.
Suggested foods: Garlic, ginger, orange or lemon peel or scallions.

Shred

Place shredding disc into container. Pack food into feed tube vertically for short shreds; pack food horizontally for longer shreds.
Suggested foods: Potatoes, onions, carrots, Cheddar cheese, American cheese, Mozzarella cheese, Swiss cheese, cabbage, zucchini, or coconut as shown.

Slice

Place slicing disc into container. Pack food into feed tube. Process using light pressure for thin slices. Press harder for thick slices. To slice green pepper, remove top from pepper, halve it and remove seeds. Insert pepper through bottom of the feed tube, stem side up, gently squeezing pepper to make it fit. Slice. If the pepper is small enough, leave it whole, and remove seeds and pith through the top.
Suggested foods: Cooked or raw meat, carrots, zucchini, pepperoni, breakfast sausage, hot dogs, pickles, olives, cucumbers, celery, potatoes, mushrooms, onions, radishes, eggplant, lettuce, strawberries, apples, lemons, limes, pears, bananas, tomatoes.

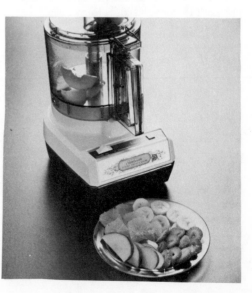

Mix

Place steel cutting blade into container. Place all ingredients except liquids which you may wish to add through feed tube while the machine is running. Process briefly. Use TOUCH/ON control to finish processing. DO NOT OVERPROCESS.

Suggested foods: Cookie dough, quick breads, cake batters, pastry.

Dice

Place French-fry cutter into container. Place vegetables into feed tube horizontally. Slice thickly. Place slicing disc into container. Pack sliced food vertically into feed tube through the bottom of the feed tube. Slice again.

Machine-chopped vegetables cannot be cut uniformly enough in size and shape to be used for an attractive display, but if you wish to use them in soup or stew, they would be adequately diced.

Suggested foods: Potatoes, green pepper, cucumbers, zucchini, thick carrots, large beets.

HINTS FOR BEST USE OF YOUR FOOD PROCESSOR

☐ Assemble all ingredients and utensils near the food processor before you begin. Measure ingredients, clean and precut foods to feed tube size, if necessary.

☐ Plan ahead to save on clean up. Dry ingredients need a dry bowl, so process them first, then continue with foods that have more moisture, such as vegetables and fruits. Finally, process fatty foods like cheeses and meats. Rinse the container after processing each food, only when necessary. Wash thoroughly at the end.

☐ When processing several different kinds of fruits or vegetables, prepare each type separately even if they are to be combined, since there will be differences in textures.

☐ *Be careful not to overprocess.* Overprocessing is easily done because the food processor works so fast. Don't hesitate to turn the unit OFF and look at the food you are processing. You can always process a little longer if the food isn't fine enough. For greater control, you may wish to use the TOUCH/ON control.

☐ When mixing liquids or batters using the cutting blade, DO NOT remove the blade before lifting the processing container from the base. This should help to avoid liquids spilling down the center hole and onto the base of the unit. Pour liquid ingredients from the processing container, using a spatula to press against the center of the blade to hold it in place.

☐ When cutting shortening into sugar or flour, it is advisable to use TOUCH/ON control for ON/OFF action to obtain a more even blend.

☐ When processing yeast dough, the motor may slow down because the dough has become so sticky and rubbery. If this happens, add ¼ cup flour, 1 tablespoon at a time, using the TOUCH/ON control to blend the flour in. Add more flour, if necessary, until the motor comes to speed again.

☐ In general, the ideal size for processing is about 1" square — *never* larger than about 1½". The harder the food the smaller the pieces needed for effective processing.

☐ Most foods can be processed 2½ cups at a time. If you have larger amounts to process, divide the ingredients.

☐ If any food items should become caught between the blade and the side of the bowl, turn the processor off and wait until the blades stop turning. Then remove the cover and lift the blade to free the food item.

☐ During the processing of some recipes, the blade may become "locked" on the center shaft of the mixing container. To remove the blade, unplug the unit from the electrical outlet and grasp the grip on the top of the blade. Carefully rock the blade back and forth, rotating it on the shaft until the blade is freed.

☐ The container, cover, pusher, blade, and disc may be washed in warm, soapy water, rinsed thoroughly, and dried. Or they may be washed in an automatic dishwasher. Place items on the top rack of the dishwasher, away from the heating element. Avoid the use of abrasive cleansers and cleaning pads.

NOTE: Handle the blades and discs very carefully as they are extremely sharp.

☐ **PLEASE READ THE INSTRUCTIONS THAT COME WITH YOUR FOOD PROCESSOR.**

CONVERTING RECIPES FOR FOOD PROCESSING

Many recipes in your files or cookbooks can be adjusted to let the food processor help speed preparation. Check first to see if there is a similar one in this book. If so, follow the steps taken. The Food Processor Guide can tell you which blade or disc to use. The Food Processing Equivalent Chart gives you the amounts of food you will have after they have been processed.

Most recipes in this book list ingredients in the order of processing rather than use. In converting your recipe, rearrange the ingredients so that the crumbing, chopping, slicing, mincing, and grating procedures are done first. Follow with blending, creaming, and mixing. So that you can see how easily this is done, we have converted the meat loaf recipe shown below:

ORANGE MEAT LOAF   Yield: Serves 4

¾ cup bread crumbs
½ cup orange juice
1 pound ground beef
½ slice bacon, cut fine
1 tablespoon grated orange rind
½ teaspoon salt

¼ teaspoon each, pepper and garlic salt
⅛ teaspoon powdered basil
½ cup chopped onion
¼ cup chopped parsley
Orange slices

Preheat oven to 350°F. Mix bread crumbs with orange juice. Combine with remaining ingredients except orange slices. Shape into a loaf. Place in a pan. Bake 1 hour. Garnish with orange slices.

Here is the same recipe for use with a food processor:

1½ slices bread
2 oranges
1 small onion, cut into quarters
½ cup loosely packed fresh parsley
½ slice bacon

1 pound beef cubes
½ teaspoon salt
¼ teaspoon each, pepper and garlic salt
⅛ teaspoon powdered basil

Place steel cutting blade into the container. Crumb 1½ slices bread. Remove. Place slicing disc into the container. Slice an orange. Set slices aside. Squeeze juice of another orange. Mix orange juice and bread crumbs. Place steel cutting blade into the container. Grate orange rind. Chop 1 small onion. Chop ½ cup parsley. Chop sliced bacon. Chop 1 pound beef.

Combine all ingredients except orange slices. Shape into loaf. Place in 9" loaf pan. Bake 30 minutes at 350°F. Garnish with orange slices. Makes 4 servings.
Notice that the order of processing was planned for rinsing the container as little as possible.

FOOD PROCESSING EQUIVALENTS

Type of Food	Amount	Desired Processing Result	Approximate Yield
Apple	1 medium (5 to 6 oz.)	Shredded or thick strips	1 cup
		Sliced	½ to ¾ cup
		Chopped	½ cup
Banana	1 medium (6 oz.)	Sliced thin	1 cup
		Mashed	½ cup
Beets	3 medium (2 oz. ea.) cooked or raw	Shredded	1½ cups
		Sliced	2 cups
Bread	1 slice fresh (3½-in. sq.)	Crumbed	½ cup
	1 slice dry (3½-in. sq.)	Crumbed	⅓ cup
Cabbage	¼ medium head	Chopped	¾ to 1 cup
		Sliced or shredded	1½ to 2 cups
Carrots	1 medium	Chopped, sliced, or shredded	½ to ¾ cup
Celery	2 stalks	Coarsely chopped or sliced	½ to ¾ cup
Cheeses	hard (½ lb.) (Parmesan)	Finely chopped	1¾ to 2 cups
	soft (2 oz.) (Mozzarella)	Shredded	½ cup
	Cheddar, Swiss (4-oz. piece)	Sliced	12 slices

Type of Food	Amount	Desired Processing Result	Approximate Yield
Coconut	3 oz., fresh	Chopped	⅔ to 1 cup
	1 small (4" diameter)	Shredded coarsely	2½ cups
Cookies			
Ginger snaps	17	Chopped to crumbs	1 cup
Chocolate wafers	24	Chopped to crumbs	1¼ cups
Vanilla wafers	33	Chopped to crumbs	1¼ cups
Crackers			
Graham	16 squares	Chopped to crumbs	1¼ cups
Saltines	28 squares	Chopped to crumbs	1 cup
Zwieback	8 slices	Chopped to crumbs	1 cup
Cucumber	1 medium (6" x 1½")	Shredded	1 cup
		Sliced	1½ cups
Eggs	1 hard-cooked	Chopped	⅔ to ¾ cup
Green Pepper	1 medium	Chopped, shredded, or sliced	¾ to 1 cup
Leeks	2 medium	Chopped or sliced	⅓ to ½ cup
Meat	8 oz., lean	Chopped	1 cup
		Sliced	¾ to 1 cup
Mushrooms	12 medium or 6 large	Chopped or shredded	1 cup
		Sliced	1¼ cups

Type of Food	Amount	Desired Processing Result	Approximate Yield
Nuts			
Almonds, Walnuts and Pecans	1 cup	Chopped fine	¾ to 1 cup
Peanuts	2 cups	Puréed to nut butter	2 cups
Onions			
Dry	1 medium	Chopped or sliced	½ cup
Green	1 medium	Chopped	1 tablespoon
Parsley, fresh	1 cup, loosely packed	Chopped	⅔ to 1 cup
Potatoes	1 medium	Sliced	¾ cup
	1 medium	Chopped or shredded	½ cup
Shallots	5 to 6 whole	Chopped	¼ cup
Squash			
Acorn	1 medium	Chopped, coarse to fine	1½ to 2 cups
		Sliced	2 to 3 cups
Butternut	1 medium	Chopped	1⅓ to 2 cups
		Sliced	3 cups
Zucchini or Yellow	1 medium	Chopped, fine	1 to 1¼ cups
		Sliced	2 cups
Tomatoes	1 medium (2½" diameter)	Chopped or sliced	¾ cup
Strawberries	12 medium	Sliced	1⅓ cups

FOOD PROCESSING GUIDE

Processing Task	Recommended Blade or Disc	General Processing Instructions	Suggested Foods
Blend	Steel Cutting Blade	Place all ingredients into processing container. You may wish to add liquid ingredients through the feed tube. Process until smooth.	salad dressings, dips, sauces, spreads, gelatins, milk shakes, flavored butters
Chop	Steel Cutting Blade	Foods, such as meat, should be precut into 1" cubes. Place all ingredients into processing container. Process, using TOUCH/ON control, until desired consistency.	parsley, raw meat, nuts, mushrooms, cooked meat, carrots, cabbage, hard-cooked eggs, corn chips, olives, pickles, pimiento, tomatoes
Crumb	Steel Cutting Blade	*For fine crumbs:* While food processor is running, drop pieces of food down feed tube. Continue processing until desired consistency. *For larger crumbs:* Place pieces of food into processing container. Process using TOUCH/ON control, until desired consistency.	graham crackers, saltine crackers, vanilla wafers, chocolate wafers, gingersnaps, dry or fresh bread
Dice	French-fry Cutter Disc Slicing Disc	Place French-fry cutter disc into container. Place vegetables into feed tube horizontally. Slice thickly. Place slicing disc into container. Pack slices vertically into feed tube through the bottom. Slice again.	potatoes, green pepper, cucumbers, zucchini, thick carrots, large beets
Grate	Steel Cutting Blade	Foods should be cut into 1" cubes. (Hard cheeses should be at room temperature.) Place all ingredients into container. Process, using TOUCH/ON control, until desired consistency.	hard cheeses such as Parmesan or Romano

Processing Task	Recommended Blade or Disc	General Processing Instructions	Suggested Foods
Julienne	Slicing Disc	Slice food as directed in SLICE section. Pack sliced food lengthwise horizontally into feed tube. Process.	potatoes, carrots
Knead	Steel Cutting Blade	Place ingredients into processing container. (You may wish to add liquid ingredients through feed tube.) Process, just until dough ball forms. DO NOT OVERPROCESS.	bread dough
Mince	Steel Cutting Blade	While food processor is running, drop food down feed tube. Food minces very quickly.	garlic, green onions
Mix	Steel Cutting Blade	Place all ingredients into processing container. (You may wish to add liquid ingredients through feed tube.) Process a few seconds. Use TOUCH/ON control to finish processing. DO NOT OVER-PROCESS.	cookie dough, quick breads, cake batters, pastry
Purée	Steel Cutting Blade	Place all ingredients into processing container. Process until smooth.	fresh, cooked, or canned fruits (such as peaches, bananas, apples, pears, strawberries)

fresh, cooked, or canned vegetables (such as carrots, beans, potatoes, corn, peas, tomatoes) |

Processing Task	Recommended Blade or Disc	General Processing Instructions	Suggested Foods
Shred	Shredding Disc	Pack food into feed tube. Process. Note: For shorter shreds, pack food vertically into feed tube. For longer shreds, pack food horizontally into feed tube.	potatoes, onions, carrots, Cheddar cheese, American cheese, Mozzarella cheese, Swiss cheese, cabbage, zucchini, coconut
Slice	Slicing Disc	Pack food into feed tube. Process. Note: Use light pressure on food pusher for thinner slices. Use firm pressure for thicker slices. For longer slices, pack food horizontally into feed tube. For shorter slices, pack food vertically into feed tube.	cooked or raw meat, carrots, zucchini, cucumbers, celery, potatoes, mushrooms, onions, radishes, strawberries, apples, lemons and limes, pears, bananas, tomatoes, pepperoni, breakfast sausage, hot dogs, pickles, olives, eggplant, lettuce

THE APPETIZER TABLE

Chapter One

A little something before the meal to tempt the appetite helps relax the guests and encourages sociability. You can relax, too, if you do as much of the preparation as possible in advance. The food processor can help to make the spreads and dips, shred the cheese, mince the corned beef, and slice the frankfurters. Hot hors d'oeuvres must be fried, broiled, baked, or heated in the microwave oven just before serving, but   this takes just a few minutes, and you're soon back to join in the fun.

CORN PUPPIES   Yield: Serves 10 to 12

Crisply fried frankfurter slices that go well with beverages served before dinner. The slicing disc does this job nicely.

Oil for frying
8 frankfurters, slightly frozen
1¼ cups sifted all-purpose flour, divided
⅔ cup yellow cornmeal
2 tablespoons granulated sugar

1½ teaspoons baking powder
1 teaspoon salt
2 tablespoons vegetable oil
1 egg, well beaten
¾ cup milk

Heat oil to desired temperature in deep fryer. Place slicing disc into container. Slice frankfurters. Empty into a small bowl. Add ¼ cup flour. Toss to coat frankfurters with flour. Place steel cutting blade into container. Add remaining flour, cornmeal, sugar, baking powder, and salt. Process to mix ingredients. Add vegetable oil, egg, and milk. Process until blended. Skewer 3 frankfurter pieces with a toothpick. Coat with batter. Drop a few at a time, into hot oil. Fry until golden brown on each side; about 1 minute. Serve hot.

CREAM CHEESE-LEEK DIP   Yield: About 1 cup

1 (8-ounce) package cream cheese,
   cut into 8 chunks

3 tablespoons sour cream
4 to 5 teaspoons leek soup mix

Place steel cutting blade into container. Add cream cheese. Process until smooth. Add sour cream. Process until creamy. Add leek soup mix and process to blend. Chill for at least 1 hour before serving. Serve with raw vegetables or potato chips.

CREAMY CHEDDAR SPREAD   Yield: About 1½ cups

4 ounces mild Cheddar cheese
2 (3-ounce) packages cream cheese,
   cut into chunks

1 teaspoon chopped chives
⅛ to ¼ teaspoon garlic powder

Place shredding disc into container. Shred Cheddar cheese. Empty onto a piece of waxed paper. Place steel cutting blade into container. Add Cheddar and cream cheeses. Process until smooth. Add chives and garlic powder. Process until well blended. Serve with crackers at room temperature.

DEVILED HAM AND CREAM CHEESE SPREAD   Yield: Serves 6 to 8

1 (8-ounce) package cream cheese, softened
1 (4½-ounce) can deviled ham
2 tablespoons sweet pickle relish

¼ teaspoon onion salt
¼ teaspoon garlic salt

Place steel cutting blade into container. Add all ingredients to container. Process until blended. Serve chilled on crackers or breads.

GUACAMOLE   Yield: 2 cups

This zippy Mexican avocado dip is quickly mixed with the steel blade.

2 tablespoons onion
2 tablespoons canned, green chili peppers
2 ripe avocados, peeled and quartered
1 medium tomato, peeled and quartered

1½ tablespoons lemon juice
1 teaspoon salt
⅛ teaspoon white pepper
Dash of cumin

Place steel cutting blade into container. Add onion and chili peppers. Process until finely chopped. Add avocados, tomato, and process until smooth and creamy. Add lemon juice, salt, white pepper, and cumin. Process until well blended. Serve chilled as a dip with crackers, chips, or vegetables.

LIVER SAUSAGE AND BACON SPREAD   Yield: 1 cup

8 ounces liver sausage
1 tablespoon butter or margarine, softened
½ teaspoon Worcestershire sauce

3 tablespoons bacon bits
1 teaspoon minced onion

Place steel cutting blade into container. Process liver sausage, butter, Worcestershire sauce, bacon bits, and onion until well blended. Remove cover and scrape down container sides. Chill for ½ hour in separate container. Serve with crackers.

ONION-CHEESE-BACON SPREAD   Yield: Serves 4 to 6

1 tablespoon butter or margarine, melted
2 tablespoons mayonnaise
½ small onion, peeled and quartered
Dash of seasoned salt

4 ounces processed American cheese,
  broken into pieces
4 slices crisp, cooked bacon,
  broken into pieces

Place steel cutting blade into container. Add butter, mayonnaise, onion, and seasoned salt. Process until thoroughly blended. Drop cheese and bacon down feed tube and process until blended. Remove cover and scrape down container sides, as necessary. Spread on bread or hamburger buns. Broil until cheese is melted. Serve hot.

ONION DIP   Yield: Serves 10 to 12

6 sprigs parsley
½ cup mayonnaise
1 cup sour cream

1 cup cottage cheese
¼ cup dehydrated onion soup mix

Place steel cutting blade into container. Add parsley sprigs. Process until finely chopped. Add remaining ingredients and process until smooth and thoroughly blended. Serve chilled with melba toast, potato chips, or crackers.

PIMIENTO-OLIVE-CHEESE BALLS   Yield: About 25 balls

Olives are the surprise inside the cheese crust. These are ambrosial morsels.

4 ounces sharp Cheddar cheese
2 tablespoons butter or margarine, softened
½ cup sifted all-purpose flour
⅛ teaspoon dry mustard

Dash of white pepper
Dash of paprika
25 small pimiento-stuffed green olives,
  well drained

Preheat oven to 400°F. Grease a cookie sheet. Place shredding disc into container. Shred cheese. Empty cheese onto waxed paper. Place steel cutting blade into container. Add shredded cheese and butter. Process until smooth. Remove cover and scrape down container sides. Add flour, dry mustard, white pepper, and paprika. Process until dough ball forms. Remove dough by teaspoonfuls. Roll into balls. Flatten each ball to ⅛" thickness. Wrap around an olive, covering completely. Seal edges. Place onto prepared cookie sheet. Bake for 10 to 15 minutes, or until bottoms are golden brown. Serve warm.

REUBEN BALLS   Yield: 30 to 36 balls

Corned beef meat balls that are full-flavored tempters.

1 medium onion, peeled and quartered
1 clove garlic, peeled
2 tablespoons butter or margarine
1 pound sliced corned beef, cut into pieces
5 parsley sprigs
2 cups sauerkraut, drained

½ cup sifted all-purpose flour
1 beef bouillon cube
½ cup hot water
2 ounces Swiss cheese
2 slices bread, cut into pieces
2 eggs

Place steel cutting blade into container and chop onion and garlic. In a frypan, sauté onion and garlic in butter until tender. Place steel cutting blade into container and mince corned beef. Add minced corned beef to onion and cook for 5 minutes. Place steel cutting blade into container and chop parsley and sauerkraut. Add parsley, sauerkraut, and flour to corned beef mixture. Dissolve bouillon cube into hot water and pour over corned beef mixture. Cook for 10 to 15 minutes, stirring often. Place shredding disc into container and shred Swiss cheese. Spread cooked corned beef mixture onto a cookie sheet. Sprinkle with Swiss cheese and refrigerate 1 hour. Heat oil to desired temperature in a deep fryer. Place steel cutting blade into container and add bread. Use TOUCH-ON control to make bread crumbs. Empty onto waxed paper. In a small bowl, beat eggs. Shape corned beef mixture into 1" balls. Roll balls into beaten eggs and then bread crumbs. Fry, a few at a time, until golden brown. Drain on paper towels. Serve hot.

SCALLION-CREAM CHEESE SPREAD   Yield: Serves 4 to 6

1 scallion, cut into chunks
1 tablespoon milk

1 (8-ounce) package cream cheese,
  cut into chunks

Place steel cutting blade into container. Add scallion. Process until finely chopped. Add milk and cream cheese. Process, using TOUCH-ON control, until smooth. Chill before serving. Serve with crackers or bagels.

VEGETABLE DIP   Yield: 1 cup

2 scallions cut into chunks
2 sprigs parsley
1 (8-ounce) package cream cheese,
  cut into chunks

½ cup mayonnaise or salad dressing
1 teaspoon dill weed
1 teaspoon Italian seasoning

Place steel cutting blade into container. Chop scallions and parsley. Remove cover. Add cream cheese, mayonnaise, dill weed, and Italian seasoning. Process until well blended. Serve with fresh vegetables.

FRENCH-FRIED ONION CHEESE BALL   Yield: About 2 cups

Here is an attractive way to serve a cream cheese mixture that tastes good, too.

1 (3-ounce) can French fried onions
2 (8-ounce) packages cream cheese, cut
  into chunks
2 teaspoons celery salt

1 teaspoon paprika
1 teaspoon Worcestershire sauce
Walnut half or one cherry (optional)

Place steel cutting blade into container. Coarsely crush French fried onions. Empty onto a sheet of waxed paper. Place steel cutting blade into container. Add cream cheese, celery salt, paprika, and Worcestershire sauce. Process until smooth and creamy. Add crushed French fried onions, reserving ¼ cup for topping. Process only until blended. Turn mixture onto a sheet of waxed paper and shape into a ball. Roll ball into reserved French fried onions to coat cheese. Top with a walnut half or cherry, if desired.

Variation: Blend entire can of French fried onions into cream cheese. Use chopped nuts for topping.

ASSORTED CHEESE ROUNDS   Yield: Serves 8 to 10

These most appetizing hot cheeses on party rounds are easily accomplished with your food processor to shred cheese and chop scallions.

3 ounces mild Cheddar cheese
3 ounces Swiss cheese
3 ounces Parmesan cheese cut into chunks

4 scallions, cut into chunks
33 slices party rye
¼ cup salad dressing

Place shredding disc into container. Shred Cheddar cheese. Empty onto a sheet of waxed paper. Place shredding disc into container. Shred Swiss cheese. Empty onto a separate sheet of waxed paper. Place steel cutting blade into container. Add Parmesan cheese. Process, using TOUCH-ON control, until cheese is grated. Empty onto a sheet of waxed paper. Place steel cutting blade into container. Add scallions. Process until finely chopped. Spread each slice of party rye with salad dressing. Top with chopped scallions. Sprinkle shredded Cheddar cheese over 11 pieces of bread; shredded Swiss over 11, and grated Parmesan over 11. Place on ungreased cookie sheet. Broil until cheese is bubbly. Serve hot.

AVOCADO-BLUE CHEESE DIP   Yield: Serves 8 to 10

1 ripe avocado, peeled and quartered
2 tablespoons lemon juice
1 tablespoon onion
¼ cup light cream
4 ounces cream cheese, softened and cut
    into chunks

4 ounces blue cheese, softened and cut
    into chunks
3 drops Tabasco sauce
1 teaspoon celery seed
Dash of salt
1 to 2 drops green food coloring (optional)

Place steel cutting blade into container. Add avocado, lemon juice, and onion. Process until well blended. Remove cover and scrape down container sides. Add cream, cheeses, Tabasco sauce, celery seed, salt, and food coloring, if desired. Process until smooth. Serve chilled as a dip with crackers, chips, or fresh vegetables.

CHEDDAR STUFFED CELERY   Yield: Serves 8 to 10

A tangy cheese mixture in crisp, cold celery stalks.

1 medium bunch of celery
8 ounces sharp Cheddar cheese
¼ cup mayonnaise

¾ teaspoon dry mustard
Dash of Tabasco sauce

Remove leaves from celery. Wash and dry each stalk. Cut into 2" lengths. Place shredding disc into container and shred cheese. Empty cheese onto waxed paper. Place steel cutting blade into container. Process cheese, mayonnaise, dry mustard, and Tabasco sauce until smooth. Fill celery pieces with cheese mixture. Serve chilled.

CHICKEN-CHEESE SPREAD   Yield: Serves 3 to 4

2 ounces Cheddar cheese
1½ cups cooked chicken,
    cut into 1" pieces

1 teaspoon dill weed
3 tablespoons mayonnaise

Place shredding disc into container and shred cheese. Empty cheese onto waxed paper. Place steel cutting blade into container and process until chicken is coarsely chopped. Remove cover and add cheese, dill weed, and mayonnaise. Process until mixture is blended. Serve chilled on crackers or breads.

CHOPPED LIVER   Yield: Serves 3 to 4

1 medium onion, peeled and quartered
½ pound cooked chicken livers

2 hard-cooked eggs, peeled and quartered
2 to 3 tablespoons chicken fat

Place steel cutting blade into container. Add onion. Process until coarsely chopped. Add chicken livers. Process, using TOUCH-ON control, until coarsely chopped. Add eggs. Process, using TOUCH-ON control, until finely chopped. Empty into a small bowl. Add chicken fat. Blend with fork. Serve chilled with crackers or rye bread.

CLUB CHEDDAR CHEESE SPREAD   Yield: Serves 10 to 12

1 (2¼-ounce) can deviled ham
1 tablespoon Worcestershire sauce
½ teaspoon dry mustard

Dash of cayenne pepper
12 ounces Cheddar cheese, cubed
½ cup milk

Place steel cutting blade into container. Add deviled ham, Worcestershire sauce, dry mustard, and cayenne pepper. Process until smooth. Alternately drop cheese cubes and milk down feed tube as unit runs. Process until smooth. Remove cover and scrape down container sides, as necessary. Serve chilled on crackers, breads, or vegetables.

Variation: Form mixture into a ball. Chill for several hours, before rolling in chopped nuts or parsley. Serve immediately with crackers, breads, or vegetables.

BLUE CHEESE DIP   Yield: Serves 8 to 10

1 (8-ounce) package cream cheese,
  cut into chunks
1 (3-ounce) package cream cheese,
  cut into chunks

1 (4-ounce) package blue cheese, crumbled
½ cup sour cream
¼ teaspoon garlic salt
¼ teaspoon onion salt

Place steel cutting blade into container. Add cream cheese and blue cheese. Process until smooth. Add sour cream, garlic and onion salts. Process until creamy. Chill for at least 1 hour before serving. Serve with raw vegetables, potato chips, or use to top baked potatoes.

THE SOUP POT

Chapter Two

Making soups from scratch is easy with a food processor to do the chopping, slicing, or purée-ing of vegetables. The processor does such a fine job that every bit of the vegetable's flavor is retained. In this chapter you'll find a variety of soups. Some are meant to be served hot, others cold; some hearty, others light. The spicy aroma of soup bubbling on the stove can truly make a house a home.

CREAM OF CARROT SOUP   Yield: Serves 3 to 4

For a change of pace, serve this soup chilled with a dollop of sour cream.

6 to 8 medium carrots, peeled
   and cut into 1" pieces
1 onion, peeled and quartered
⅓ cup butter or margarine
1 cup chicken stock, divided
2 whole cloves

1½ cups milk, divided
2 tablespoons sifted all-purpose flour
½ cup water
½ cup heavy cream
Salt and pepper

Place steel cutting blade into container. Finely chop carrots and onion. Melt butter in frypan. Sauté carrots and onion in butter until onion is wilted. Add ½ cup chicken stock and cloves. Cook until carrots are tender. Remove cloves. Place steel cutting blade into container. Put carrot mixture, 1 cup milk, and flour into container. Process until smooth. Pour into saucepan. Stir in remaining milk, water, and chicken stock. Cook over low heat, about 10 minutes, stirring constantly. Add cream. Season to taste. Serve immediately.

VEGETABLE SOUP   Yield: Serves 6 to 8

Any vegetables except beets, which give it too much color, may be used for this soup.

8 cups water
3 bouillon cubes
2 whole bay leaves
1 teaspoon thyme
2 pounds beef cubes
3 medium celery stalks

3 medium carrots, peeled
2 medium potatoes, peeled and quartered
1 small onion, peeled and quartered
½ green pepper, cut into chunks
1 (16-ounce) can tomatoes

In a 6-quart pan, combine water, bouillon cubes, bay leaves and thyme. Cover pan and simmer 1 hour. Add beef cubes and continue to simmer for 1 hour, or until beef cubes are tender. Place slicing disc into container. Slice the celery, carrots, and potatoes. Remove the vegetables to a large bowl filled with cold water. Place the steel cutting blade into the container. Coarsely chop the onion and green pepper. When beef cubes are tender, remove the bay leaves. Add the sliced celery, carrots, potatoes, chopped onion, green pepper, and canned tomatoes. Continue to simmer soup for 30 minutes until vegetables are tender. Serve hot.

CHICKEN VEGETABLE SOUP   Yield: Serves 3 to 4

½ cup cubed, cooked chicken
2 carrots, peeled and cut into pieces
1 medium stalk celery, cut into pieces

1 small onion, peeled and quartered
3 sprigs parsley
2 cups seasoned chicken broth

Place steel cutting blade into mixing container. Process chicken, carrots, celery, onion and parsley until finely chopped. Add chicken broth and process just long enough to thoroughly mix ingredients. Turn into saucepan and simmer for 1 hour, until vegetables are cooked.

FRENCH ONION SOUP   Yield: Serves 8 to 10

A French soup that is an American favorite.

3 pounds red onions, peeled and halved
¾ cup butter or margarine
6 beef bouillon cubes
2 quarts water
1 cup dry white wine
1 teaspoon Worcestershire sauce

1 teaspoon salt
Dash of white pepper
Dash of black pepper
8 ounces chilled Swiss or Gruyère cheese
½ loaf French bread

Place slicing disc into container. Slice onions. Melt butter in a 4-quart Dutch oven. Slowly cook onions in butter until lightly browned, about 20 minutes. Add bouillon cubes, water, and wine to onions. Cover and simmer 2 hours, stirring occasionally. Add Worcestershire sauce, salt, white and black peppers to soup. Stir. Place shredding disc into container. Shred cheese. To serve soup, place a thin slice of French bread into the bottom of each individual ovenware serving bowl. Ladle soup into bowls. Top with a thick layer of shredded cheese. Place under broiler until cheese melts. Serve at once.

CREAM OF MUSHROOM SOUP   Yield: Serves 3 to 4

More delicious than the canned soup, and just as easy when you have a food processor.

2 tablespoons butter or margarine
1 small onion, peeled and quartered
2 stalks celery, cut into 1" chunks
4 ounces fresh mushrooms
2 cups milk, divided

2 tablespoons sifted all-purpose flour
½ teaspoon salt
¼ teaspoon onion salt
¼ teaspoon pepper

In a saucepan, melt butter. Place steel cutting blade into container. Coarsely chop onion and celery. Pour into saucepan. Place slicing disc into container. Slice mushrooms. Add to onion and celery mixture. Sauté until tender. Place steel cutting blade into container. Add 1 cup milk, flour, salt, onion salt, pepper, and sautéed vegetables to container. Process until mushrooms are finely chopped. Pour back into saucepan. Stir in remaining cup of milk. Heat until thickened. Serve warm.

GAZPACHO   Yield: Serves 5 to 6

This Spanish soup is strong tasting and zesty. Prepare it 6 to 8 hours before serving to be sure it's ice cold.

1 small onion, peeled and quartered
2 cloves garlic, peeled
3 green peppers, cored and quartered
4 tomatoes, peeled, quartered,
    and seeded
1 large cucumber, peeled
    and cut into chunks
Dash of salt

Dash of pepper
½ teaspoon chili powder
⅓ cup olive oil
¼ cup lemon juice
3 cups tomato juice
¼ cup dry sherry
½ cup sour cream

With steel cutting blade in container, process each of the first 5 ingredients, separately, until chopped. Pour into a large jar. Add salt, pepper, chili powder, olive oil, lemon juice, tomato juice, and sherry to jar. Stir to blend. Chill thoroughly. Serve cold with a dollop of sour cream.

CREAM OF CELERY SOUP   Yield: Serves 5 to 6

A mild, thick soup, pleasing to the palate.

1 medium onion, peeled and quartered
⅓ cup butter or margarine
2 medium potatoes, peeled
    and cut into 1" pieces
6 stalks celery
1 cup water

½ bay leaf
½ teaspoon salt
¼ teaspoon black pepper
2 cups milk, divided
8 sprigs parsley

Place steel cutting blade into container. Coarsely chop onion. Sauté in saucepan, in butter, until golden brown. Place steel cutting blade into container. Add potatoes. Process until coarsely chopped. Empty into saucepan with onions. Place slicing disc into container. Slice celery. Empty into saucepan with potatoes and onion. Add water, bay leaf, salt, and pepper to saucepan. Cover and cook slowly 30 minutes, or until vegetables are soft. Remove bay leaf. Place steel cutting blade into container. Add 1 cup milk, and half the cooked vegetables. Process until smooth. Add parsley. Process until chopped. Empty mixture into small mixing bowl. Repeat with remaining mixture. Return to saucepan. Heat slowly until thickened and serve hot.

SPLIT PEA SOUP   Yield: Serves 6 to 8

A wonderful supper dish. It can be reheated and served with good bread and butter, salad and assorted cheeses.

1 cup split peas, sorted and washed
2 quarts cold water, divided
⅛ teaspoon baking soda
1 stalk celery, cut into chunks
1 small carrot, peeled and cut into chunks
½ medium onion

2 slices bacon
2 sprigs parsley
¼ bay leaf
1 tablespoon butter or margarine
Salt and pepper

In a Dutch oven or a large saucepan, soak peas overnight in 1 quart water and baking soda. The next morning, drain the peas and add 1 quart fresh water to peas. Place steel cutting blade into container. Add celery, carrot, onion, bacon, and parsley. Process until finely chopped. Add to peas, along with bay leaf and butter. Cover and simmer 3 to 4 hours. Cool slightly. Place steel cutting blade into container. Pour soup into container, 2 cups at a time, and process until smooth. Season to taste. Reheat before serving.

VICHYSSOISE   Yield: Serves 6 to 8

This classic cold soup is a variation of the popular potato and leek soup.

5 medium potatoes, peeled
   and cut into 1" cubes
4 cups boiling water
6 chicken bouillon cubes
¼ cup butter
2 medium onions, peeled and quartered

1 cup heavy cream
1 cup milk
1 teaspoon salt
¼ teaspoon pepper
Chopped chives
Paprika

Combine potatoes, water, bouillon cubes, butter, and onions. Cover and cook until the potatoes are very tender, about 30 minutes. Drain, reserving liquid. Place steel cutting blade into container. Process the drained vegetables, ½ at a time, until very smooth. Return vegetables to their cooking liquid. Add cream, milk, salt, and pepper. Stir. Chill thoroughly. Serve cold, garnished with chopped chives and paprika. (Soup may also be reheated and served hot.)

MINESTRONE SOUP   Yield: Serves 4 to 6

This Italian specialty can easily serve as the main course. Top with a heavy sprinkling of Parmesan.

2 cups water
2 beef bouillon cubes
2 large carrots, peeled
    and cut into chunks
2 medium celery stalks with tops,
    cut into chunks
1 medium onion, peeled and quartered
1 small zucchini

1 clove garlic, peeled
1 (8-ounce) can tomatoes with liquid
½ (6-ounce) can tomato paste
1 can kidney beans, drained
1½ teaspoons parsley flakes
1 teaspoon salt
¼ teaspoon black pepper
2 ounces spaghetti, broken into 2" pieces

In a large saucepan or Dutch oven, heat water to a boil. Add bouillon cubes. Place steel cutting blade into container. Add carrots, celery, and onion. Process until finely chopped. Add to heated mixture. Place shredding disc into container. Shred zucchini. Add zucchini to heated mixture, along with garlic. Cover and cook for 5 minutes. Reduce heat to simmer. Cut tomatoes into chunks. Add tomatoes and tomato liquid, tomato paste, kidney beans, parsley flakes, salt, and pepper. Cook for 1½ hours. Stir occasionally. Adjust temperature to medium heat and add spaghetti. Cook for 30 minutes. Serve hot.

OLD-FASHIONED CHEDDAR CHEESE SOUP   Yield: Serves 5 to 6

The sharper and more aged the cheese you use in this soup, the better it is.

6 ounces Cheddar cheese
¾ cup carrots, cooked
2 medium stalks celery,
    cut into 1" pieces
2 medium scallions

¼ cup sifted all-purpose flour
1 teaspoon salt
½ teaspoon pepper
4 cups milk, divided
¼ cup butter or margarine

Place shredding disc into container. Shred cheese. Empty onto waxed paper. Place steel cutting blade into container. Add carrots, celery, scallions, flour, salt, and pepper. Process until finely chopped. Add 1½ cups milk. Process for 3 to 4 seconds. Pour into saucepan. Stir in remaining 2½ cups milk and butter. Cook over medium heat, stirring constantly, until slightly thickened. Lower heat and add cheese, ½ cup at a time. Stir until cheese melts. Serve warm.

THE SALAD BAR

Chapter Three

The food processor is a master at salad making. Its skillful chopping, slicing, and shredding gives you beautiful results with little effort. With the hard work done for you, why not be adventurous in combining foods for salads. There is an infinite variety of possibilities. Dressings are child's play with the food processor's help, and in seconds you can have a new and different combination for every meal. This chapter has a large variety of salads and dressings to get you started.

MAKE YOUR OWN SALAD   Yield: Serves 6

Let your guests put their salads together from an assortment of salad ingredients. It makes them feel at home, and allows for individual preferences.

1 medium head lettuce, torn into pieces
3 hard-cooked eggs, peeled and halved
1 pound bacon, cooked
¼ pound mushrooms
3 stalks celery, cleaned

1 small onion, peeled
1 green pepper, cored and halved
3 carrots, peeled
Parsley (optional)

Place torn lettuce into a large salad bowl. Place steel cutting blade into container. Coarsely chop eggs. Begin preparing a salad accompaniment tray by placing chopped egg in a section of tray. Place steel cutting blade into container. Coarsely chop bacon. Place chopped bacon in a section on tray. Place slicing disc into container. Slice mushrooms. Place mushrooms on tray. Do the same for celery, onion, and green pepper. Place shredding disc into container. Shred carrots and place on tray. Garnish with parsley, if desired. Provide your guests with their own individual salad bowls. Allow them to prepare their own salads. Serve with favorite salad dressings.

WILTED LETTUCE SALAD   Yield: Serves 6 to 8

1 head lettuce, cut into wedges
½ teaspoon salt
3 slices bacon
1 small onion, peeled

½ cup white vinegar
1 tablespoon granulated sugar
1 hard-cooked egg, sliced

Place slicing disc into container. Slice lettuce. Place into preheated 2½-quart serving dish. Sprinkle lettuce with salt and let stand 10 minutes. Meanwhile, fry bacon in a frypan until crisp. Drain on paper towels. Place slicing disc into container. Slice onion. Add onion to bacon drippings in frypan. Cook over medium heat until tender. Add vinegar and sugar to frypan. Continue heating until bubbly. Drain lettuce. Pour vinegar mixture over lettuce. Crumble bacon over all. Stir with a fork to blend. Garnish with egg slices. May be served hot or cold.

CREAMY CAULIFLOWER LETTUCE SALAD   Yield: Serves 10 to 12

Raw cauliflower gives crunch to this salad. Layer in a clear glass or plastic bowl until you're ready to toss.

1 small head fresh cauliflower
1 medium head iceberg lettuce,
   cut into wedges
½ pound cooked bacon, crisp, drained

1¼ cups mayonnaise
½ cup granulated sugar
½ cup grated Parmesan cheese
1 small onion, quartered

In a large bowl, break cauliflower into bite-sized pieces. Set aside. Place slicing disc into container. Slice lettuce. Dry with paper toweling and layer over cauliflower. Place steel cutting blade into container. Add bacon. Process, using TOUCH-ON control, until coarsely chopped. Place on paper toweling. Place steel cutting blade into container. Add mayonnaise, sugar, Parmesan cheese, and onion. Process until onion is coarsely chopped, about 5 seconds. Pour mixture over lettuce. Sprinkle with chopped bacon. Cover bowl and refrigerate 2 to 4 hours. Toss lightly before serving.

SUMMER GARDEN SALAD   Yield: Serves 3 to 4

Here is a crisp green salad that can be made ahead.

4 cups torn lettuce
½ head cauliflower,
   broken into flowerets
3 to 4 stalks celery

20 radishes
1 green pepper, cored
1 to 2 ounces blue cheese

Place lettuce into salad bowl. Place slicing disc into container. Slice all vegetables and arrange in bowl with torn lettuce. Place steel cutting blade into container. Add blue cheese. Process, using TOUCH-ON control, until crumbly. Sprinkle over salad.

Suggested Dressing: Italian Dressing (see page 64).

TUNA-SHOESTRING SALAD   Yield: Serves 4 to 6

This is tuna fish salad with a difference. Arrange on a bed of lettuce and surround with cherry tomatoes and black olives.

4 carrots, peeled	1 cup mayonnaise
2 stalks celery, cut into 1" pieces	3 tablespoons ketchup
1 small onion, peeled and quartered	2 tablespoons granulated sugar
1 (7-ounce) can tuna, drained	1 (6-ounce) can shoestring potatoes

Place shredding disc into container. Shred carrots. Empty carrots onto waxed paper. Place steel cutting blade into container. Add celery, onion, tuna, and shredded carrots. Process until coarsely chopped. Empty mixture into a large bowl. Place steel cutting blade into container. Add mayonnaise, ketchup, and sugar. Process until dressing is smooth. Pour over tuna mixture and stir until moistened. Refrigerate for 2 to 4 hours, to blend flavors. Remove from refrigerator. Stir in shoestring potatoes. Serve immediately.

THREE BEAN SALAD   Yield: Serves 8 to 10

A California creation, bean salads have many variations. This one is good served with cold meats or fish.

1 (1-pound) can kidney beans, drained	3 stalks celery, cut into 1" pieces
1 (1-pound) can wax beans, drained	1 cup granulated sugar
1 (1-pound) can cut green beans, drained	1 cup cider vinegar
1 small onion, peeled and quartered	½ cup salad oil
½ green pepper, quartered	2 teaspoons salt

In a large bowl, add kidney, wax, and green beans. Place steel cutting blade into container. Add onion, green pepper, and celery. Process until coarsely chopped. Add chopped onion mixture to beans. Place steel cutting blade into container. Add sugar, vinegar, salad oil, and salt. Process until all ingredients are well blended. Pour dressing over beans. Toss lightly. Refrigerate overnight. Serve on salad greens.

EGG SALAD   Yield: Serves 3 to 4

A favorite for luncheons.

1 medium stalk celery,
   cut into 1" chunks
6 hard-cooked eggs, peeled and halved

¼ cup salad dressing
¼ teaspoon salt
Dash of pepper

Place steel cutting blade into container. Add celery. Process until coarsely chopped. Add eggs. Process, using TOUCH-ON control, until eggs are coarsely chopped. Add salad dressing, salt, and pepper. Process, using TOUCH-ON control, until just blended. Chill before serving.

VEGETABLE MEDLEY SALAD   Yield: Serves 10 to 12

½ cup granulated sugar
½ teaspoon celery seed
½ teaspoon salt
½ clove of garlic, finely chopped
¾ cup cider vinegar
1 medium-sized head cabbage, cut into wedges

4 medium-sized carrots, peeled
1 green pepper, cored and seeded
3 large stalks celery
1 small onion, peeled
2 small, firm tomatoes

In a medium saucepan, combine sugar, celery seed, salt, garlic, and vinegar. Heat, stirring occasionally, until sugar is dissolved. Set aside to cool. Place shredding disc into container. Shred cabbage. Empty cabbage into a large bowl. Shred carrots and add to cabbage. Place slicing disc into container. Slice green pepper, celery, onion, and tomatoes. Add to cabbage mixture. Toss lightly with a fork. Pour cooled dressing over cabbage mixture and toss again. Chill in refrigerator for at least 2 hours or overnight. Drain sauce before serving.

CARROT-RAISIN SALAD   Yield: Serves 4 to 6

Delicious and nutritious with pineapple and coconut to give it a Hawaiian flavor.

1 (8-ounce) can pineapple chunks,
   drained
8 medium carrots, peeled
½ cup raisins

¼ cup shredded coconut
⅓ cup mayonnaise or salad dressing
2 teaspoons lemon juice

Place steel cutting blade into container. Coarsely chop pineapple. Empty into small bowl. Place shredding disc into container. Shred carrots. Add shredded carrots, raisins, coconut, mayonnaise, and lemon juice to pineapple. Toss lightly. Serve immediately.

CHICKEN SALAD Yield: Serves 3 to 4

There are many opinions about what chicken salad should be. Here is a traditional receipe that is simple and elegant.

3 stalks celery, cut into 1" chunks
3 sweet pickles
6 spanish olives
4 hard-cooked eggs,
  peeled and quartered

½ teaspoon salt
2 cups cubed, cooked chicken
1 to 2 tablespoons mayonnaise
Lettuce leaves

Place steel cutting blade into container. Add celery, pickles, olives, and eggs. Process, using TOUCH-ON control, until coarsely chopped. Add salt, chicken, and mayonnaise. Process until ingredients are mixed. DO NOT OVERPROCESS. Serve chilled on lettuce leaves.

CRABMEAT SALAD IN TOMATO CUPS Yield: Serves 4

A beautiful presentation of a savory salad.

4 large stalks celery, cut into 1" pieces
½ medium green pepper,
  cored and cut into chunks
1 small onion, peeled and quartered
⅔ cup sour cream
⅓ cup mayonnaise

1 tablespoon lemon juice
½ teaspoon Worcestershire sauce
½ teaspoon salt
1 (7½-ounce) can crabmeat, flaked
4 large tomatoes, chilled
Dash of paprika

Place steel cutting blade into container. Add celery, green pepper, and onion. Process until finely chopped. Add sour cream, mayonnaise, lemon juice, Worcestershire sauce, and salt. Process until blended. Empty into a large bowl. Fold in crabmeat. Cover and refrigerate 30 minutes. Slice each tomato into wedges without cutting all the way through the tomato. Gently fan out wedges to form a flower. Spoon chilled crabmeat into center of tomato. Sprinkle with paprika. Serve immediately.

OLD-FASHIONED COLESLAW   Yield: Serves 6 to 8

The food processor may be the single greatest cause of coleslaw's reawakened popularity. It's actually a pleasure to shred cabbage.

COLESLAW

½ medium head of cabbage,
   cut into wedges

1 medium carrot

Place slicing disc into container. Slice cabbage. Empty into a large bowl. Place shredding disc into container. Shred carrot. Empty into bowl with cabbage.

DRESSING

1 cup mayonnaise
¼ cup sour cream
2 tablespoons white vinegar
1 teaspoon prepared mustard

1 teaspoon granulated sugar
1 teaspoon salt
½ teaspoon paprika

Place steel cutting blade into container. Add all ingredients. Process until well blended. Pour over cabbage. Toss. Refrigerate 2 to 4 hours. Serve chilled.

MARINATED SAUERKRAUT SALAD   Yield: Serves 10 to 12

This pungent salad will be the perfect companion to pork, ham, and sausages.

⅓ cup salad oil
1¼ cups granulated sugar
½ cup cider vinegar
⅓ cup water
1 green pepper, cored and quartered

3 large stalks celery
4 medium carrots, peeled
1 small onion, peeled
2 (16-ounce) cans sauerkraut,
   drained and rinsed

In a medium saucepan, combine salad oil, sugar, vinegar, and water. Heat, stirring occasionally, until the sugar dissolves. Cool. Place slicing disc into container. Slice green pepper, celery, carrots, and onion. Pour into a large bowl. Add sauerkraut and toss lightly. Add cooled sauce mixture and toss again. Refrigerate overnight. Drain before serving.

FRESH MUSHROOM SALAD   Yield: Serves 6 to 8

A happy combination of marinated mushrooms and spinach or watercress.

1 pound fresh mushrooms	1½ teaspoons granulated sugar
¼ small green pepper	½ teaspoon salt
2 sprigs parsley	⅛ teaspoon black pepper
1 tablespoon chopped chives	½ teaspoon dill weed
1½ teaspoons tarragon leaves	2 teaspoons prepared mustard
5½ tablespoons lemon juice	½ cup bottled Italian dressing
¼ cup pimiento	1 small bunch spinach or watercress

Place slicing disc into container. Slice mushrooms and green pepper. Empty into a large bowl. Place steel cutting blade into container. Add parsley, chives, tarragon, and lemon juice. Process until finely chopped. Add to mushroom mixture. Cover and refrigerate 30 minutes. Place steel cutting blade into container. Add pimiento, sugar, salt, pepper, dill weed, mustard, and Italian dressing. Process until well mixed. Cover and refrigerate 30 minutes. Arrange spinach leaves on a large platter. Pour dressing over mushroom mixture. Toss to coat. Spoon onto spinach leaves. Serve immediately.

WALDORF SALAD   Yield: Serves 8 to 10

This gustatory delight puts your food processor to some of its finest tasks.

¾ cup shelled walnuts	½ cup raisins
6 medium apples, cored	½ cup miniature marshmallows (optional)
and cut into 1" chunks	½ cup mayonnaise or salad dressing
4 stalks celery	2 teaspoons lemon juice

Place steel cutting blade into container. Coarsely chop walnuts. Empty into large bowl. Process apple chunks, until coarsely chopped. Add to walnuts. Place slicing disc into container and slice celery. Add celery, raisins, marshmallows, and lemon juice to apple mixture. Toss lightly. Add mayonnaise. Toss to coat apples. Serve immediately on lettuce leaves.

Variation: For variety, apples may be sliced.

CUCUMBERS AND ONIONS IN SOUR CREAM   Yield: Serves 4 to 6

This is a staple salad relish. Substitute yogurt for sour cream if you're watching calories.

2 large cucumbers, peeled
1 small onion, peeled
1½ cups sour cream
2 tablespoons cider vinegar

1 tablespoon granulated sugar
½ teaspoon salt
Dash of black pepper

Place slicing disc into container. Slice cucumbers and onion. Empty into a small bowl. Separate onion into rings. Place steel cutting blade into container. Add sour cream, vinegar, sugar, salt, and pepper. Process until well blended, about 5 to 10 seconds. Pour sauce over cucumbers and onions. Stir. Chill before serving.

SOUR CREAM-APPLE AND RAISIN COLESLAW   Yield: Serves 6 to 8

Choose this coleslaw to serve with pork.

1 large head of cabbage,
  cut into wedges
1 medium, tart, red apple, cored
  and quartered
1½ cups sour cream
2 egg yolks

2 tablespoons lemon juice
1 teaspoon prepared horseradish
¼ teaspoon paprika
1½ teaspoons granulated sugar
1 teaspoon salt
⅓ cup raisins

Place slicing disc into container. Slice cabbage. Empty into large bowl. Place steel cutting blade into container. Add apple. Process until coarsely chopped. Add to cabbage. Place steel cutting blade into container. Add sour cream, egg yolks, lemon juice, horseradish, paprika, sugar, and salt. Process until well blended. Pour over cabbage mixture. Add raisins. Toss until well coated. Refrigerate at least 30 minutes before serving.

TOSSED ZUCCHINI SALAD   Yield: Serves 6 to 8

A combination of crunchy vegetables and a pungent dressing with an affinity for seafood dishes.

SALAD

1 small head Romaine lettuce
1 small head Boston lettuce
2 medium zucchini

1 cup radishes
½ cup cauliflower

Tear Romaine and Boston lettuce into bite-sized pieces and place in salad bowl. Place slicing disc into container. Slice zucchini, radishes, and cauliflower. Add to salad greens. Chill.

DRESSING

2 scallions, cut into chunks
⅓ cup salad oil
3½ tablespoons tarragon vinegar

1 teaspoon salt
1 clove garlic, peeled and crushed
¼ teaspoon black pepper

Place steel cutting blade into container. Add scallions, oil, vinegar, salt, garlic, and pepper. Process until well blended. Refrigerate for 30 minutes. Pour over chilled salad greens. Toss until vegetables are coated. Serve immediately.

APPLESAUCE   Yield: Serves 4 to 6

4 large apples, peeled, cored,
   and quartered
½ cup water

½ cup granulated sugar
½ teaspoon cinnamon

Place slicing disc into container and slice apples. Place apple slices in a saucepan and add water. Simmer until apple slices are tender. Drain off water. Place steel cutting blade into container. Add cooked apple slices, sugar, and cinnamon. Process until smooth. Serve hot or cold.

UNCOOKED APPLESAUCE   Yield: Serves 3 to 4

A tartly sweet sauce to serve with poultry or pork entrees.

4 large apples, peeled, cored,
   and quartered
3 tablespoons honey

¼ teaspoon cinnamon
¼ cup water

Place steel cutting blade into container. Add apples, honey, cinnamon, and water. Process until puréed. Serve immediately.

SUNSHINE PEARS   Yield: Serves 4 to 6

6 firm, medium-sized pears,
   cored and halved

4 cups water
Approximately ½ cup granulated sugar

Place slicing disc into container. Slice pears and empty into a large saucepan. Add water and sugar to taste. Cook over medium heat 45 to 60 minutes, or until tender. May be served warm or cold.

LAYERED FRESH FRUIT SALAD   Yield: Serves 10 to 12

1 honeydew melon, peeled
   and cut into wedges
1 cantaloupe, peeled
   and cut into wedges

1 pineapple, remove rind and eyes, and cut
   into lengthwise wedges
2 bananas, peeled
1 pint strawberries, hulled
½ pint blueberries

Place steel cutting blade into container. Slice each fruit separately, then layer separately in a large glass bowl. Garnish with blueberries, if desired. Serve immediately.

Serving Suggestion: Serve with Celery Seed Dressing (see page 64) or Fruit and Honey Dressing (see page 62).

Hint: Chill all fruit before slicing.

DOUBLE STRAWBERRY MOLD   Yield: Serves 4

1 (3-ounce) package strawberry gelatin
½ pint fresh strawberries, hulled

Whipped topping (optional)
Whole strawberries (optional)

Prepare gelatin according to package directions, using 1 cup boiling water and 1 cup cold water. Refrigerate until it begins to thicken. Place slicing blade into container. Slice strawberries. Fold sliced strawberries into thickened gelatin. Pour into 4 individual molds or into a 3-cup mold. Refrigerate until firm. Unmold and garnish with whipped topping and whole strawberries, if desired.

RASPBERRY WALDORF MOLD   Yield: Serves 6 to 8

1 (6-ounce) package raspberry gelatin
2 cups boiling water
2 cups cold water

3 stalks celery
3 apples, cored and cut into 8 wedges
½ cup chopped walnuts

In a large bowl, dissolve gelatin in 2 cups boiling water. Add 2 cups cold water and stir. Refrigerate 4 hours, or until firm. Place slicing disc into container. Slice celery and empty onto waxed paper. Slice apples and empty onto a separate sheet of waxed paper. Place steel cutting blade into container. Add chilled raspberry gelatin. Process, using TOUCH-ON control, until gelatin is whipped. Add sliced celery and process, using TOUCH-ON control, until just blended. Add sliced apples and nuts and process, using TOUCH-ON control, until combined. Pour into a 6-cup mold. Chill until set. Unmold onto a platter.

CREAMY LEMON MOLD   Yield: Serves 6 to 8

2 (3-ounce) packages lemon gelatin
2 cups boiling water
½ cup granulated sugar
1 (6-ounce) can frozen lemonade
  concentrate

9 ounces frozen whipped topping
Additional frozen whipped topping
  (optional)
1 lemon, sliced (optional)

In a large bowl, dissolve gelatin in boiling water. Add sugar and lemonade concentrate. Stir until dissolved. Refrigerate until set. Place steel cutting blade into container. Add chilled gelatin. Process, using TOUCH-ON control, until gelatin is whipped. Remove cover. Add a quarter of whipped topping. Process, using TOUCH-ON control, until well blended. Continue adding remaining quarters of whipped topping in the same manner. Pour into a 6-cup mold. Chill until set, approximately 3 to 4 hours. Unmold onto platter. Garnish with whipped topping and lemon slices, if desired.

VINAIGRETTE   Yield: 1 cup

¼ cup red wine vinegar
¾ teaspoon prepared mustard
¾ cup olive oil

Dash of salt
Dash of pepper

Place steel cutting blade into container. Combine all ingredients. Process using the TOUCH-ON control, until ingredients are thoroughly blended.

THOUSAND ISLAND DRESSING Yield: About 2 cups

2 sprigs parsley
Several celery leaves
¼ medium green pepper
½ small onion, peeled and quartered
1 cup mayonnaise

⅓ cup ketchup
1 hard-cooked egg, peeled and quartered
¼ cup sweet pickle relish
¼ teaspoon salt
2 drops Tabasco sauce

Place steel cutting blade into container. Add parsley, celery leaves, green pepper, and onion. Process until coarsely chopped. Add remaining ingredients. Process until well blended. Pour into a separate container. Cover and refrigerate overnight. Serve over salad greens.

QUICKIE THOUSAND ISLAND DRESSING Yield: About 2 cups

1 hard-cooked egg, shelled
  and quartered
1 medium dill pickle or sweet pickle,
  quartered

1½ cups salad dressing
½ cup ketchup
1 to 2 tablespoons granulated sugar

Place steel cutting blade into container. Add egg. Process until coarsely chopped. Empty onto a sheet of waxed paper. Place steel cutting blade into container. Add pickle. Process until coarsely chopped. Empty onto a sheet of waxed paper. Place steel cutting blade into container. Add salad dressing, ketchup, and sugar. Process until well blended. Add chopped egg and pickle to container. Process just until combined. Chill. Serve over salad greens.

FRUIT AND HONEY DRESSING Yield: 1¼ cups

1 (8-ounce) container plain,
  lowfat yogurt

2 tablespoons honey
¼ cup fresh or frozen fruit

Place steel cutting blade into container. Combine yogurt, honey, and fresh fruit. Process until thoroughly blended. Serve over fresh fruit.

AVOCADO DRESSING Yield: 1¼ cups

½ cup orange juice
½ lemon, peeled and seeded
¼ teaspoon salt

2 teaspoons mayonnaise
1 avocado, peeled, quartered, and seeded

Place steel cutting blade into container. Add all ingredients. Process until smooth. Pour into a separate container. Cover and refrigerate. Serve chilled over salad greens.

BLUE CHEESE OR ROQUEFORT DRESSING Yield: 2 cups

1 cup evaporated milk
½ cup salad oil
¼ cup vinegar

½ teaspoon salt
Dash of garlic salt
½ cup crumbled blue or Roquefort cheese

Place steel cutting blade into container. Add all ingredients. Process until mixture is smooth. Pour into a separate container. Cover and refrigerate overnight. Serve over salad greens.

CREAMY GARLIC DRESSING Yield: 2 cups

2 cloves garlic, peeled
2 cups sour cream
1 teaspoon salt

½ teaspoon granulated sugar
½ teaspoon paprika
¼ teaspoon white pepper

Place steel cutting blade into container. Add garlic. Process, using TOUCH-ON control, to mince garlic. Add remaining ingredients to container. Process until well blended. Pour into a separate container. Cover and refrigerate overnight. Serve over salad greens.

RUSSIAN DRESSING Yield: About 2 cups

½ cup condensed tomato soup
⅓ cup white vinegar
¾ cup salad oil
½ clove garlic, peeled
½ small onion, peeled and halved

½ cup granulated sugar
1 teaspoon dry mustard
1 tablespoon Worcestershire sauce
½ teaspoon paprika
1 teaspoon salt

Place steel cutting blade into container. Add all ingredients to container. Process until thoroughly blended. Pour into a separate container. Cover and refrigerate overnight. Serve over salad greens.

SOUR CREAM DRESSING Yield: 1½ cups

½ carrot, peeled and cut into 1" chunks
3 scallions, cut into 1" chunks
1 cup sour cream
¼ cup mayonnaise or salad dressing

1 teaspoon lemon juice
½ teaspoon celery seed
¼ teaspoon salt
Dash of seasoned salt

Place steel cutting blade into container. Add carrot and scallions. Process until finely chopped. Add remaining ingredients. Process until well blended. Pour into a separate container. Cover and refrigerate overnight. Serve over salad greens.

ITALIAN DRESSING   Yield: 1½ cups

2 cloves garlic, peeled
1 cup salad oil
3 tablespoons lemon juice
3 tablespoons white vinegar
1 teaspoon salt
1 teaspoon granulated sugar

½ teaspoon crushed oregano
½ teaspoon dry mustard
½ teaspoon onion salt
¼ teaspoon paprika
Dash of thyme

Place steel cutting blade into container. Add garlic. Process, using TOUCH-ON control, to mince garlic. Add remaining ingredients to container. Process until well blended. Pour into separate container. Cover and refrigerate overnight. Before serving, shake lightly. Serve over salad greens.

APRICOT-HONEY DRESSING   Yield: 2 cups

1 (1-pound) can apricots, drained
¼ lemon, peeled and seeded
1 strip lemon rind (1" x 2")

¼ cup honey
¼ teaspoon salt
1 cup sour cream

Place steel cutting blade into container. Add apricots, lemon, and rind. Process until apricots are puréed. Add honey, salt, and sour cream. Process only until well mixed. Serve over fresh fruit.

Variation: Substitute 1 (1-pound) can of peaches for the apricots.

CELERY SEED DRESSING   Yield: 1⅓ cups

½ cup salad oil
½ cup honey
¼ cup cider vinegar

½ teaspoon celery seed
½ teaspoon salt

Place steel cutting blade into container. Add all ingredients to container. Process until well blended. Serve chilled on fruit salads.

MAYONNAISE   Yield: 1¼ cups

1 egg
¾ teaspoon salt
½ teaspoon dry mustard
¼ teaspoon paprika

1 tablespoon white vinegar
1 tablespoon lemon juice
1 cup salad oil, divided

Place steel cutting blade into container. Add egg, salt, dry mustard, paprika, vinegar, lemon juice, and ¼ cup of oil. Process, while *slowly* adding remaining oil drop-by-drop through feed tube. Continue to process until all of the oil has been added.

THE MAIN-DISH MEDLEY

Chapter Four

This chapter has a mixture of main dishes of varied origins—American as well as foreign recipes. Many have been avoided by people too busy to cook. Now, with the food processor's help, they can be reintroduced as possibilities for everyone to try.

BEEF STROGANOFF   Yield: Serves 5 to 6

This delicious Russian dish depends on two things for its effect — the thinness of the meat and the fresh taste that shows it was completed immediately before serving.

6 tablespoons butter or margarine,
  divided
3 scallions
1 pound fresh mushrooms
2 pounds lean beef, partially frozen,
  cut into chunks

½ cup dry white wine
1 teaspoon Worcestershire sauce
1 teaspoon Dijon-style mustard
Salt and pepper to taste
1 cup sour cream
Hot cooked noodles

In a frypan, melt 3 tablespoons butter. Place slicing disc into container. Slice scallions. Add to frypan. Sauté until tender. Meanwhile, slice mushrooms. Add to frypan. Cook over medium heat until lightly browned. Place slicing disc into container. Slice beef. In a large frypan, heat remaining butter. Add beef slices. Cook until just browned. Turn meat to simmer. Add wine, cooked mushroom mixture, Worcestershire sauce, mustard, salt, and pepper. Cook for 1 minute. Add sour cream. Cook until just warm. Do *not* allow mixture to boil as sour cream will curdle. Serve immediately over hot cooked noobles.

CORNED BEEF SPREAD   Yield: Serves 4 to 6

A savory sandwich idea.

2 (3-ounce) packages corned beef slices,
  cut into pieces
¼ cup mayonnaise

1 stalk celery, cut into pieces
1 tablespoon sweet pickle relish
1 teaspoon caraway seed

Place steel cutting blade into container. Add corned beef, mayonnaise, and celery. Process just until mixture is coarsely chopped. Pour into a large bowl. Stir in pickle relish and caraway seed. Serve hot or cold as a sandwich filling.

Serving Suggestion: Serve with Mustard Butter (see page 123) and Swiss cheese on rye bread. Grill the sandwiches until each side is golden brown and cheese has melted.

BEEF AND MUSHROOM RATATOUILLE   Yield: Serves 8 to 10

2½ pounds beef, partially frozen
   and cut into chunks
¼ cup salad oil
3 medium onions, peeled and quartered
1 clove garlic, peeled
1 (1-pound 12-ounce) can tomatoes
1 tablespoon oregano

1 teaspoon salt
½ teaspoon black pepper
1 pound fresh mushroom caps
1 medium eggplant, peeled
   and cut into chunks
2 zucchini, ends trimmed

Place slicing disc into container. Slice beef. In a Dutch oven or large saucepan, heat 2 tablespoons oil. Add half of the meat and cook over medium heat until browned. Remove from pan. Repeat procedure for remaining oil and meat. Meanwhile, place steel cutting blade into container. Add onions and garlic. Process until finely chopped. Remove beef from pan and add onion mixture. Cook until tender. Return beef to pan, along with tomatoes, oregano, salt, and pepper. Heat to boiling; then reduce heat, cover, and simmer for 90 minutes. Stir occasionally. Place slicing disc into container. Slice mushrooms. Add to heated mixture. Place slicing disc into container. Slice eggplant and add to heated mixture. Place slicing disc into container. Slice zucchini and add to heated mixture. Cover and simmer 30 minutes, or until vegetables are tender, stirring occasionally. Serve hot.

SLOPPY JOES   Yield: Serves 4 to 6

A popular ground beef sandwich, its name may be a forewarning of its tendency to drip.

1 pound ground beef
1 small onion, peeled and quartered
½ small green pepper, quartered
¾ cup chili sauce

1 teaspoon Worcestershire sauce
2 teaspoons brown sugar
Salt and pepper to taste

In a large frypan, brown ground beef over medium heat. Drain off excess fat. Place steel cutting blade into container. Add onion and green pepper. Process until coarsely chopped. Add onion mixture to ground beef and continue cooking until onion is tender. Add chili sauce, Worcestershire sauce, brown sugar, salt, and pepper to ground beef. Simmer for 5 to 10 minutes. Serve hot as a sandwich filling.

SPICY MEATBALLS   Yield: Serves 10 to 15

Serve over noodles. Make your own salad (see page 51)' and for the grand finale, Strawberry Shortcake (see page 139). Your party will be a sure-fire success.

MEATBALLS

2 pounds ground beef
2 slices bread
1 teaspoon oregano
1 large onion, peeled and quartered
1 clove garlic, peeled
1 medium green pepper, cored
   and quartered

6 sprigs parsley
1 teaspoon Worcestershire sauce
1 egg
½ teaspoon salt
¼ teaspoon freshly ground
   black pepper

Crumble beef into a large bowl. Place steel cutting blade into container. Add bread and oregano. Process until bread crumbs are formed. Add to ground beef. Place steel cutting blade into container. Add onion, garlic, green pepper, and parsley. Process until coarsely chopped. Add to ground beef. Add Worcestershire sauce, egg, salt, and pepper to ground beef. Stir until thoroughly combined. Shape into 2″ balls and brown in a frypan over medium heat. Drain excess grease from frypan.

Serving Suggestion: Serve with Spicy Sauce (see page 154).

QUICK TACOS   Yield: 5 servings

From south of the border—hot and spicy.

1 pound ground beef
1 (1¼-ounce) package taco seasoning mix
4 ounces Cheddar cheese
½ head iceberg lettuce, cut into wedges

2 medium tomatoes, quartered
1 package prepared taco shells
Taco sauce (optional)

In frypan, brown ground beef. Drain fat. Add taco seasoning mix. Prepare beef as directed on taco seasoning package. Empty into dish. Place shredding disc into container. Shred cheese. Empty into a serving dish. Place slicing disc into container. Slice lettuce. Empty into a serving dish. Place steel cutting blade into container. Coarsely chop tomatoes using TOUCH-ON control. Empty into a serving dish. Assemble tacos by layering meat, cheese, tomatoes, and lettuce in individual taco shells. Serve with taco sauce, if desired.

CHICKEN WITH MUSHROOM SAUCE   Yield: Serves 2 to 3

Simple, but it gives your chicken a touch of class.

½ pound fresh mushrooms
2 (10½-ounce) cans cream of mushroom
  soup

⅓ cup milk
⅓ cup red cooking wine
1 (2½- to 3-pound) cut-up fryer

Preheat oven to 375°F. Place slicing disc into container. Slice mushrooms. Empty onto a piece of waxed paper. Place steel cutting blade into container. Add soup, milk, and wine. Process until well blended. Add sliced mushrooms. Process, using TOUCH-ON control, just until mushrooms are combined. Place chicken in an ungreased 13" x 9" x 2" pan, skin side up. Pour soup mixture over chicken. Bake for 1 hour, or until tender. Serve immediately.

CRISPY PARMESAN CHICKEN   Yield: Serves 2 to 3

A marvelous coating for chicken made easily in your food processor.

¼ to ½ cup butter or margarine
1 clove garlic, peeled
1 ounce Parmesan cheese, cut in 1" cubes
2 slices bread, quartered
2 tablespoons almonds

2 sprigs parsley
1 teaspoon salt
¼ teaspoon poultry seasoning
Dash of black pepper
1 (2½- to 3-pound) cut-up fryer

Preheat oven to 400°F. Place butter in a 13" x 9" x 2" pan. Place steel cutting blade into container. Add garlic. Process until minced. Add to butter. Place pan in oven to melt butter. Place steel cutting blade into container. Process Parmesan cheese until grated. Add bread. Process until crumbed. Add almonds. Process until chopped. Add parsley, salt, poultry seasoning, and pepper. Process until parsley is chopped. Empty container onto a piece of waxed paper. Remove pan from oven. Dip chicken pieces into butter, then coat with crumb mixture. Place into pan, skin side up. Bake for 1 hour, or until tender. Do not turn. Serve immediately.

STIR-FRY CHICKEN CASHEW   Yield: Serves 5 to 6

Inspired by the Chinese style of cooking meat and vegetables, this is a delicious and attractive looking dish.

4 chicken breasts, skinned and boned
  (partially frozen)
1 clove garlic, peeled
1 medium green pepper,
  cored and halved
½ pound mushrooms
¼ cup soy sauce

¾ teaspoon granulated sugar
1 tablespoon cornstarch
¾ cup chicken broth
5 tablespoons oil
3 scallions, cut into 1" pieces
Hot cooked rice
¾ cup cashew nuts

Place the slicing disc into container. Slice the chicken breasts. Empty onto a piece of waxed paper. Place steel cutting blade into container. Add garlic. Process, using TOUCH-ON control, until minced. Empty onto a sheet of waxed paper. Remove steel cutting blade from container. Place slicing disc into container. Slice green pepper and mushrooms. In a small mixing bowl, combine soy sauce, sugar, cornstarch, and chicken broth. In a frypan, heat oil. Stir-fry chicken for about 3 minutes, or until it just turns opaque. Add garlic, green pepper, mushrooms, and scallions and continue to stir-fry for about 2 minutes. Lower heat, stir in sauce, cook until sauce thickens. Serve hot over cooked rice. Sprinkle with cashew nuts.

STUFFED CABBAGE CASSEROLE   Yield: Serves 4 to 5

This is a tasty casserole, combining cabbage sliced by the food processor with meat instead of the usual practice of rolling the meat in cabbage leaves.

1 medium head cabbage, cut into
  wedges
1 (29-ounce) can tomato sauce

1½ pounds ground beef,
  browned and drained
1½ cups cooked rice

Preheat oven to 350°F. Place slicing disc into container. Slice cabbage. Empty into a large saucepan of salted water. Cook over medium heat until tender; drain well. Pour a layer of tomato sauce into a 2-quart casserole. Add a layer of cabbage, using half of the cabbage. Add a layer of sauce. Add cooked ground beef and a layer of sauce. Add rice and top with remaining cabbage. Pour remaining sauce over cabbage. Bake covered for 40 to 45 minutes. Serve immediately.

TACO CASSEROLE   Yield: Serves 5 to 6

An informal, Texas barbecue-style casserole.

12 ounces Cheddar cheese
4 cups corn chips
1 pound ground beef
1 medium green pepper, cored
    and cut into 1" pieces

1 small onion, peeled and quartered
2 small, ripe tomatoes, peeled
    and quartered
1 cup barbecue sauce
1 teaspoon chili powder

Preheat oven to 375°F. Place shredding disc into container. Shred cheese. Empty onto a sheet of waxed paper. Place steel cutting blade into container. Coarsely crush corn chips, 1 cup at a time. Empty onto a sheet of waxed paper. In a frypan, brown ground beef. Drain and set aside. Place steel cutting blade into container. Add green pepper, onion, tomatoes, barbecue sauce, and chili powder. Process until vegetables are finely chopped. Add sauce to meat in frypan. Stir. Simmer mixture for 10 minutes. In the bottom of a 2-quart rectangular pan, place half the corn chips. Cover with half of meat mixture and half of the shredded cheese. Repeat layers of corn chips and meat. Top with remaining cheese. Bake for 20 to 25 minutes. Serve immediately.

BAKED TUNA LOAF   Yield: Serves 4 to 6

Need a last-minute tuna dish? This one's delicious.

3 slices fresh bread, quartered
1 small onion, peeled and quartered
6 sprigs parsley
2 (7-ounce) cans white tuna, drained
1 egg

½ cup milk
1 tablespoon lemon juice
½ teaspoon salt
½ teaspoon dill weed

Preheat oven to 350°F. Grease an 8" x 4" x 2" loaf pan. Place steel cutting blade into container. Add bread. Process until crumbs are formed. Empty onto waxed paper. Place steel cutting blade into container. Coarsely chop onion and parsley. Add bread crumbs and all remaining ingredients to container. Process until well blended, 5 to 10 seconds. Bake in prepared loaf pan 50 to 60 minutes, or until firm. Cool in pan for 10 minutes, then remove from pan by inverting onto serving platter. Serve warm.

SHRIMP CREOLE Yield: Serves 4 to 6

Shrimp prepared this way tastes good. Just be careful not to overcook them, or they'll be tough.

1 clove garlic, peeled
2 medium onions, peeled and quartered
2 stalks celery
½ pound fresh mushrooms
¼ cup butter or margarine
2 tablespoons sifted all-purpose flour
1 teaspoon salt
⅛ teaspoon black pepper
1 tablespoon white vinegar

1½ teaspoons granulated sugar
1 bay leaf
⅛ teaspoon paprika
¼ teaspoon chili powder
4 drops Tabasco sauce
1 (28-ounce) can tomatoes with juice
1 green pepper, cored and quartered
1 pound cleaned, cooked shrimp
Hot cooked rice

Place steel cutting blade into container. Coarsely chop garlic and onions. Empty onion mixture onto waxed paper. Place slicing disc into container. Slice celery and mushrooms. Melt butter over low heat in a large frypan. Add onion mixture, celery, and mushrooms. Sauté until tender. Add flour, salt, pepper, vinegar, sugar, bay leaf, paprika, chili powder, and Tabasco sauce. Cook 5 minutes, or until mixture thickens. Add tomatoes with juice. Cover pan and simmer for 20 minutes, stirring occasionally. Place steel cutting blade into container. Chop green pepper. Add to frypan along with cooked shrimp. Cover and simmer for another 10 minutes. Serve over hot cooked rice.

SALMON PATTIES Yield: Serves 5 to 6

An excellent change from the standard fish dishes.

2 slices white bread
1 (15½-ounce) can salmon,
   broken into pieces
1 egg

2 stalks celery, cut into 1" pieces
1 small onion, peeled and quartered
6 sprigs parsley

Place steel cutting blade into container. Add bread and process to make crumbs. Add remaining ingredients. Process until mixture is combined. Shape into patties. In a lightly oiled frypan, brown patties on both sides over low heat. Serve hot.

HAM AND CHEESE TOASTIES   Yield: Serves 8 to 10

A quick an easy brunch, light lunch or supper choice. You might slice raw vegetables and make Pistachio Pineapple Dessert (see page 139) for dessert.

6 ounces Swiss cheese
1 small onion, peeled and quartered
½ green pepper, cut into chunks

1 cup fully cooked ham, cubed
⅓ cup mayonnaise
8 English muffin halves

Place shredding disc into container. Shred cheese. Empty onto waxed paper. Place steel cutting blade into container. Add onion, green pepper, and ham. Process until ingredients are coarsely chopped. Add mayonnaise and process until just blended. Spread ham mixture on English muffin halves. Top with shredded cheese. Place muffins under broiler until cheese is bubbly and toasted. Serve immediately.

ITALIAN EGGPLANT PARMIGIANA   Yield: Serves 4

This Neapolitan-style eggplant dish is a popular one. Your food processor comes to your aid by slicing the eggplant, grating the Parmesan, and shredding the Mozzarella.

1 medium eggplant, peeled and cut
  into wedges
2 ounces Parmesan cheese,
  cut into 1" cubes
8 ounces Mozzarella cheese
½ cup sifted all-purpose flour

Salt and black pepper to taste
1 egg
1 tablespoon milk
¼ cup olive oil
2 cups prepared Italian spaghetti sauce
  or tomato sauce, divided

Place slicing disc into container. Slice eggplant. Salt eggplant slices and let stand 1 hour. Meanwhile, place steel cutting blade into container. Process Parmesan cheese until finely grated. Empty onto a sheet of waxed paper. Place shredding disc into container. Shred Mozzarella cheese. Empty onto sheet of waxed paper. After 1 hour, rinse eggplant, pat dry with paper toweling. Season flour with salt and pepper. Dredge eggplant slices in seasoned flour. Mix egg and milk. In a large frypan, add olive oil and heat. Meanwhile, preheat oven to 350°F. Dip eggplant slices into egg-milk mixture. Sauté 3 to 4 minutes on each side. In a shallow 8" baking dish, pour ¼ cup tomato sauce. Cover with a layer of eggplant slices. Sprinkle with half the Parmesan cheese. Spread half the remaining tomato sauce, then half the Mozzarella cheese on top. Repeat layers with remaining sauce, eggplant, Parmesan and Mozzarella cheese. Bake for 30 minutes. Serve immediately.

CHEESE-FILLED MANICOTTI   Yield: Serves 6 to 8

With your food processor shredding, grating, and blending, this Italian casserole is easy sailing.

12 manicotti shells
½ pound Mozzarella cheese
15 ounces Ricotta cheese
1 (8-ounce) container cottage cheese
2 eggs
3 tablespoons grated Parmesan cheese
2 tablespoons whole wheat flour

4 sprigs parsley
½ teaspoon oregano
¼ teaspoon salt
⅛ teaspoon garlic powder
4 cups (1 quart) prepared spaghetti sauce
1 cup water

Preheat oven to 400°F. Prepare manicotti shells according to package directions. Set aside. Place shredding disc into container. Shred Mozzarella cheese. Empty onto a sheet of waxed paper. Place steel cutting blade into container. Add Ricotta cheese, cottage cheese, eggs, Parmesan cheese, flour, parsley, oregano, salt, and garlic powder. Process until mixture is well blended. Remove cover. Add 1 cup shredded Mozzarella cheese. Use TOUCH-ON control to blend. Heat spaghetti sauce and water in medium saucepan. Pour half of sauce into 13" x 9" x 2" baking dish. Fill individual manicotti with cheese mixture. Arrange filled manicotti in baking dish in a single layer. Top with remaining sauce, covering all manicotti. Sprinkle remaining Mozzarella cheese over sauce. Bake for 35 to 40 minutes, until cheese is lightly browned. Serve immediately.

Variation: Use Meat Sauce recipe (see page 156) for prepared spaghetti sauce.

EGGPLANT SUPREME   Yield: Serves 6 to 8

Serve this eggplant dish with a tossed green salad and Lemon Delight (see page 138). You'll please your guests.

6 tablespoons butter or margarine
1 large eggplant, peeled
1 medium onion, peeled and quartered
¼ pound fresh mushrooms
2 cups spaghetti sauce
2 teaspoons oregano

½ teaspoon salt
⅛ teaspoon black pepper
⅛ teaspoon thyme leaves
2 ounces Parmesan cheese
2 slices bread
4 ounces Mozzarella cheese

In a large frypan, melt butter. Place slicing disc into container. Slice eggplant. Add to frypan. Place steel cutting blade into container. Add onion and mushrooms. Process until coarsely chopped. Add to frypan. Sauté eggplant, onions, and mushrooms until tender. Add spaghetti sauce, oregano, salt, pepper, and thyme. Simmer for 5 to 10 minutes. Meanwhile, preheat oven to 325°F. Place steel cutting blade into container. Add Parmesan cheese. Process, while adding bread down feed tube. Continue processing until crumbs are formed. Empty onto a sheet of waxed paper. Place shredding disc into container. Shred Mozzarella cheese. Pour half of the eggplant mixture into a greased 1½-quart casserole. Sprinkle half the Mozzarella cheese and then half of the bread crumb mixture on top. Repeat layers, ending with bread crumb mixture. Bake for 15 to 20 minutes, or until bread crumbs are lightly browned. Serve immediately.

GNOCCHI VERDI   Yield: Serves 4 to 6

These little Italian green and white dumplings may be served between the antipasto and the main course, or may substitute, on occasion, for the pasta.

1 (10-ounce) package frozen spinach,
    completely defrosted, large stems
    discarded, and squeezed
    thoroughly dry
1 pound Ricotta cheese
⅔ cup Parmesan cheese, divided
1½ cups sifted all-purpose flour, divided

1 small onion, peeled and quartered
2 eggs
½ teaspoon salt
¼ teaspoon freshly ground black pepper
¼ teaspoon nutmeg
¼ cup butter or margarine, melted

Grease a 13" x 9" x 2" baking pan. In a large saucepan or Dutch oven, heat water to boiling. Meanwhile, place steel cutting blade into container. Add spinach, Ricotta cheese, ⅓ cup Parmesan cheese, 1 cup flour, onion, eggs, salt, pepper, and nutmeg. Process until well blended. Shape mixture into 1" balls. Roll in remaining flour. Gently drop 12-at-a-time into boiling water. They will sink then rise to the surface. Cook for about 6 minutes. Remove with a slotted spoon. Place into prepared pan. Keep warm while preparing others. Place steel cutting blade into container. Process remaining Parmesan cheese until finely grated. Sprinkle over warm gnocchi. Dribble with melted butter. Place under broiler, until cheese is golden brown. Serve at once.

VERMICELLI CASSEROLE   Yield: Serves 6 to 8

Vermicelli noodles combined with ground beef and vegetables and topped with cheese. A crisp cold salad completes the meal.

2 tablespoons shortening
6 ounces vermicelli noodles,
    broken into 1" pieces
1½ pounds beef, cut into 1" cubes
1 clove garlic, peeled
2 small onions, peeled
1 green pepper, cored and quartered
4 stalks celery

1 (8-ounce) can vacuum-packed
    whole kernel corn
2 teaspoons chili powder
2 teaspoons salt
2 teaspoons black pepper
1 (28-ounce) can whole tomatoes
¾ cup water
8 ounces medium sharp Cheddar cheese

In a frypan, melt shortening. Add vermicelli pieces and sauté over medium heat until lightly browned. Stir occasionally. Meanwhile, place steel cutting blade into container. Add beef cubes and garlic clove. Process, using the TOUCH-ON control, until beef is chopped. Add beef mixture to frypan. Continue cooking until meat loses its red color. Place slicing disc into container. Slice onions, green pepper, and celery. Add onion mixture to frypan along with corn, chili powder, salt, and pepper. Stir to combine. Place steel cutting blade into container. Add whole tomatoes. Process, using TOUCH-ON control twice. Then, add tomatoes and water to frypan. Stir gently. Lower temperature of frypan to simmer and cook, covered, for 25 minutes. Place shredding disc into container. Shred cheese. Sprinkle over vermicelli mixture. Cover until cheese is melted. Serve immediately.

LASAGNA   Yield: Serves 6 to 8

This is a simply delicious way to prepare wide noodles baked with cheeses and meat sauce. It's fine prepared ahead, which makes it a favorite for entertaining.

2 ounces Romano cheese, cut into cubes
3 sprigs parsley
2 eggs
3 cups Ricotta cheese

1 pound Mozzarella cheese
4 ounces Parmesan cheese, cut into cubes
8 to 10 lasagna noodles
1 recipe meat sauce (see page 156)

The night before: Place steel cutting blade into container. Add Romano cheese. Process until grated. Add parsley. Process until chopped. Add eggs. Process until beaten. Add Ricotta cheese, one cup at a time. Process, using TOUCH-ON control after each addition, until well blended. Empty into a bowl; cover and refrigerate overnight.

The next day: Place shredding disc into container. Shred Mozzarella cheese. Empty onto a piece of waxed paper. Place steel cutting blade into container. Add Parmesan cheese. Process until grated. Empty onto a piece of waxed paper. Just before sauce is ready, cook lasagna noodles according to package directions; drain, and dry well. Preheat oven to 350°F. In a 13″ x 9″ x 2″ casserole, assemble the lasagna in the following order: Thin layer of sauce, noodles (cut to fit casserole), sauce, half of Ricotta mixture, half of Parmesan cheese, half of Mozzarella cheese, sauce, noodles (cut to fit casserole), sauce, Ricotta mixture, Parmesan cheese, Mozzarella cheese, and sauce. Bake for 45 to 50 minutes. Serve hot.

ENTRÉE CRÊPES   Yield: 12 to 14 crêpes

4 eggs
½ cup milk
½ cup chicken broth

½ teaspoon salt
2 tablespoons butter or margarine, melted
1 cup sifted all-purpose flour

Place steel cutting blade into container. Add all ingredients. Process about 5 seconds, until just combined. Follow crêpemaker cooking directions or: Preheat an 8″ sloped-edge pan. Grease pan lightly. Pour a scant ¼ cup of batter into pan to coat interior. Fry until edges turn light brown and batter no longer steams. Using a fork or spatula, gently loosen edges. Remove from pan. Stack on plate.

CHEESE AND CABBAGE STRUDEL CRÊPES   Yield: Serves 6 to 8

Your food processor speeds up the preparation of the cheese and cabbage filling. Both the crêpes and the filling may be made ahead and refrigerated.

3 tablespoons butter
4 ounces Cheddar cheese
½ head cabbage
1 small onion, peeled and quartered
2 tablespoons dry bread crumbs

2 tablespoons Parmesan cheese
½ teaspoon salt
Dash of pepper
6 to 8 prepared entrée crêpes (see page 77)

Melt butter in a large frypan. Place shredding disc into container. Shred Cheddar cheese. Empty onto a sheet of waxed paper. Place shredding disc into container. Shred cabbage. Pour into frypan. Place steel cutting blade into container. Coarsely chop onion and add to cabbage. Sauté cabbage and onion until tender. Add shredded cheese and remaining ingredients. Continue cooking until ingredients are warm. Spoon onto entrée crêpes. Fold and return to frypan. Cook until lightly browned. Serve warm.

Serving Suggestion: Top with dollop of sour cream.

SWEET AND SPICY CHICKEN CRÊPES   Yield: Serves 4 to 5

This is a delectable crêpe filling.

1½ cups prepared spaghetti sauce
½ cup purple grape jam
1 small onion, peeled and quartered
1 tablespoon lemon juice
2 teaspoons Worcestershire sauce

2 teaspoons prepared mustard
¼ teaspoon salt
2½ cups cooked chicken, cut into pieces
8 prepared entrée crêpes (see page 77)

Place steel cutting blade into container. Add spaghetti sauce, jam, onion, lemon juice, Worcestershire sauce, mustard, and salt. Process until smooth. Add chicken. Using TOUCH-ON control, process for 2 to 3 seconds to blend in chicken. DO NOT OVERPROCESS. Pour into saucepan. Simmer, stirring occasionally, for 10 minutes. Spoon filling onto crêpes. Fold and serve.

Variation: Substitute leftover pork or turkey for the chicken.

BEEF AND VEGETABLE CRÊPES   Yield: Serves 4 to 6

1 pound ground beef
½ teaspoon salt
⅛ teaspoon black pepper
1 small onion, peeled and quartered
1 small carrot, peeled and cut into chunks
1 stalk celery, cut into 1" pieces

½ green pepper, cored
1 clove garlic, peeled
½ pound fresh mushrooms
1 (10½-ounce) can beef or mushroom gravy
8 prepared entrée crêpes (see page 77)

Preheat oven to 350°F. Lightly grease a 13" x 9" x 2" baking dish. In a frypan, brown ground beef. Sprinkle with salt and pepper; stir. Remove beef from frypan and discard all but 2 tablespoons grease. Place steel cutting blade into container. Coarsely chop onion, carrot, celery, green pepper, and garlic, using TOUCH-ON control for 2 to 3 seconds. Transfer vegetables to frypan. Place steel cutting blade back into container. Coarsely chop mushrooms. Add to vegetables in frypan. Sauté all vegetables until just tender. Add meat and half the can of gravy. Stir until combined. Spoon onto crêpes, fold and place in prepared baking dish. Pour remaining gravy over crêpes. Bake for 10 minutes. Serve immediately.

HOT CHICKEN CRÊPES   Yield: Serves 4 to 6

16 (2" x 1¾") saltine crackers
1 scallion, cut into chunks
1 teaspoon prepared mustard
½ teaspoon paprika
2 tablespoons dry sherry

Dash of Worcestershire sauce
½ cup mayonnaise
1½ cups cooked chicken
Butter for frying
8 prepared entrée crêpes (see page 77)

Place steel cutting blade into container. Process crackers until finely crumbed. Add scallion, mustard, paprika, sherry, and Worcestershire sauce. Process only until combined. Add mayonnaise. Using TOUCH-ON control, process until combined. Add chicken. Using TOUCH-ON control, process only until chicken is combined. Spoon about 2 tablespoons filling onto each crêpe. Fold and refrigerate to dry crêpes slightly. Melt butter in large frypan. Fry filled crêpes until brown on both sides. Serve immediately.

Variation: Substitute 1½ cups leftover cooked turkey for chicken.

CRABMEAT SALAD CRÊPES   Yield: Serves 6 to 8

2 sprigs parsley
1 scallion, cut into chunks
1 (12-ounce) package crabmeat, cooked
1 stalk celery, cut into chunks
¼ cup mayonnaise

2 teaspoons prepared horseradish
¼ teaspoon salt
¼ teaspoon white pepper
2 teaspoons lemon juice
6 to 8 entrée crêpes (see page 77)

Place steel cutting blade into container. Add parsley and scallions. Process until finely chopped. Add remaining ingredients. Process until just blended. DO NOT OVERPROCESS. Pour into small bowl. Cover and chill before serving. Spoon onto entrée crêpes. Fold and serve.

TUNA DELIGHT CRÊPES   Yield: Serves 4 to 6

16 (2" x 1¾") saltine crackers
1 stalk celery, cut into chunks
1 small onion, peeled and quartered
¼ green pepper, cored and
   cut into chunks
1 small carrot, peeled,
   cut into chunks
1 egg

1 tablespoon mayonnaise
1 (10½-ounce) can condensed cream of
   celery soup, undiluted, divided
¼ teaspoon salt
Dash of black pepper
1 (7½-ounce) can tuna, drained
4 to 6 entrée crêpes (see page 77)
Dash of paprika

Preheat oven to 350°F. Grease a 9" x 9" x 2" baking dish. Place steel cutting blade into container. Add crackers. Process until finely crumbed. Empty onto a sheet of waxed paper. Place steel cutting blade into container. Add celery, onion, green pepper, and carrot. Process, using TOUCH-ON control, until coarsely chopped. Add egg, mayonnaise, ¼ can soup, salt, and pepper. Process using TOUCH-ON control, until blended. Add tuna. Process using TOUCH-ON control just until combined, about 3 seconds. DO NOT OVERPROCESS. Spoon mixture onto crêpes. Fold and place in prepared baking dish. Bake for 15 minutes. Meanwhile, heat remaining soup. Spoon a tablespoonful of hot soup over each crêpe. Sprinkle with paprika. Serve immediately.

CHICKEN CRÊPES FLORENTINE   Yield: Serves 4 to 5

2 ounces Parmesan cheese,
   cut into 1" cubes
1 slice white bread, quartered
1 (10-ounce) package chopped spinach
1 clove garlic, peeled

1 (10½-ounce) can condensed cream of
   chicken soup, undiluted, divided
2 cups cooked chicken, cut into pieces
½ cup milk
1 hard-cooked egg, sliced
8 to 10 prepared entrée crêpes (see page 77)

Preheat oven to 350°F. Grease a 13" x 9" x 2" baking dish. Place steel cutting blade into container. Process Parmesan cheese until finely grated. With processor running, drop bread down feed tube. Process until crumbed. Add spinach, garlic, and half the soup. Process until combined, about 5 seconds. Add chicken. Using TOUCH-ON control, process for 2 to 3 seconds to blend. Spoon mixture onto crêpes. Fold and place into prepared dish. Combine remaining soup with milk. Pour over crêpes. Bake for 15 to 20 minutes. Garnish with slices of hard-cooked egg and serve.

Variation: Substitute leftover turkey for chicken.

RICH MAN'S QUICHE   Yield: Serves 6 to 8

Rich or poor, it's better to make this gourmet dish with your food processor.

6 ounces Cheddar cheese
9 slices bacon
1 large onion, peeled and quartered
2 tablespoons sifted all-purpose flour
4 eggs

2 cups light cream
1 teaspoon salt
Dash of nutmeg
Dash of paprika
1 10" baked pâte brisée (see page 106)

Preheat oven to 350°F. Place shredding disc into container. Shred cheese. Empty onto waxed paper. In a large frypan, fry bacon until crisp. Drain on paper towels until cool. Crumble and set aside. Pour drippings from the frypan, reserving 2 tablespoonfuls. Place slicing disc into container. Slice onion. Add sliced onions to frypan and cook over medium heat until lightly browned. Sprinkle flour over onion. Stir to blend. Remove from heat and set aside. Place steel cutting blade into container. Add eggs, cream, salt, nutmeg, and onion mixture. Process until combined. Sprinkle cheese over bottom of pastry shell. Pour the egg mixture over the cheese. Sprinkle bacon and paprika over top. Bake for 35 to 45 minutes, or until a knife inserted into center of quiche comes out clean. Allow to cool for 5 minutes before cutting. Serve immediately.

POOR MAN'S QUICHE Yield: Serves 6 to 8

1 unbaked 9" pastry shell (see page 104)
4 to 5 ounces Swiss cheese
½ pound fresh mushrooms
2 scallions

2 tablespoons butter or margarine
2 eggs
½ cup whole milk
¼ teaspoon salt

Preheat oven to 400°F. Bake pastry shell for 5 minutes and remove from oven. Reduce oven temperature to 375°F. Place shredding disc into container. Shred cheese. Empty onto waxed paper. Place slicing disc into container. Slice mushrooms and scallions. Melt butter in a frypan. Add sliced mushrooms and scallions. Cook until tender. Set aside. Place steel cutting blade into container. Add eggs, milk, and salt. Process until well blended. Sprinkle cooked mushroom mixture and shredded cheese over bottom of pastry shell. Pour egg mixture over mushrooms and cheese. Bake for 30 to 35 minutes, or until knife inserted into center of quiche comes out clean. Allow to cool 5 minutes before cutting. Serve immediately.

THE BAKERY SHOP

Chapter Five

Your home can have freshly-baked breads, biscuits, cookies, cakes, and pies on hand at all times. Your processor can knead your dough for Hearty Wheat Loaf, and slice apples for Apple Crisp, Apple Crumb Cake, and Apple Pie with Crumb Topping. Lay in a supply to have a well-stocked larder.

HEARTY WHEAT LOAF   Yield: 1 loaf

The processor prepares the dough for this bread very easily. This is a pleasant tasting bread. It toasts nicely, too.

1 tablespoon granulated sugar	1½ cups sifted all-purpose flour
1 package active dry yeast	2 tablespoons wheat germ
1 cup warm water (110°F)	1 teaspoon salt
½ cup dry milk	2 tablespoons frozen butter or margarine
1 cup whole wheat flour	Melted butter or margarine

In a glass measuring cup, dissolve sugar and yeast in warm water. Allow to rest for 5 minutes. Meanwhile, place steel cutting blade into container. Add dry milk, ½ cup wheat flour, 1 cup all-purpose flour, wheat germ, salt, and margarine to mixing container. While processing, pour ¼ cup of yeast mixture down feed tube. Continue to process until mixture is crumbly. Allow to rest for 2 minutes. Add the remaining whole wheat and all-purpose flours. While processing, pour remaining yeast mixture down feed tube. Continue to process until mixture forms a dough ball. Place dough into a greased bowl and roll to grease dough ball. Cover and let rise in a draft-free area for 90 minutes. Punch down and let rise 40 minutes. Remove dough from bowl and let rest on a lightly floured board for 10 minutes. Grease a 9" x 5" x 3" loaf pan. Shape dough into a loaf and place in prepared pan. Brush with melted butter. Cover and allow to rise 30 minutes. Preheat oven to 350°F. Bake for 40 to 45 minutes, or until done.

SALLY LUNN   Yield: 1 loaf

There are many recipes for Sally Lunn. This one is delicious with butter and jam.

1 package active dry yeast	¼ cup granulated sugar
⅓ cup warm water (115° to 120°F)	2 eggs
⅓ cup warm milk (80° to 85°F)	2½ cups sifted all-purpose flour
⅓ cup butter or margarine, softened and cut into pieces	1 teaspoon salt

Grease a large, glass bowl. In a glass measuring cup, combine yeast in warm water. Set aside for 5 minutes. Add milk to yeast mixture. Place steel cutting blade into container. Add butter and sugar. Process until creamy. Add eggs. Process until well blended. Add flour and salt. While processor is running, pour yeast mixture down feed tube. Process until batter is smooth. Spoon into prepared bowl. Cover and let rise in a warm, draft-free area about 2 hours, or until doubled. Grease a 10" tube pan. Spoon batter into prepared pan. Cover and let rise for 1 hour. Preheat oven to 350°F. Bake for 40 to 50 minutes. Remove from pan and cool on wire rack.

BRIOCHE   Yield: 1 large loaf

Here is a popular recipe adapted to your food processor.

1 package active dry yeast
¼ cup warm milk (110°F)
1 tablespoon granulated sugar
2 cups + 2 tablespoons sifted
    all-purpose flour

1¼ teaspoons salt
½ cup frozen butter, cut
    cut into 8 pieces
2 eggs, beaten

In a measuring cup, dissolve yeast in warm milk. Add sugar and set aside. Place steel cutting blade into container. Add flour, salt, and butter. Process until crumbly. Add yeast mixture and process until combined, about 10 seconds. Add beaten eggs. Process until dough ball is formed. Place in a greased, glass bowl. Roll to grease dough ball. Cover and let rise in a warm place, until doubled, about 1½ to 2 hours. Remove a small portion of dough. Form into a teardrop shape. Form the rest of the dough into a ball. Place large ball into lightly buttered brioche pan. Make hole in center of ball and insert teardrop-shaped ball of dough. Cover and let rise until doubled, about 1 hour. Preheat oven to 350°F. Mix egg yolk and cream in a bowl. Brush onto loaf. Bake for 35 to 40 minutes, or until golden brown. Turn out of pan. Cool on wire rack.

FRENCH BREAD   Yield: 1 loaf

This long, crusty bread is marvelous spread with garlic butter and warmed.

1 package active dry yeast
1 cup warm water (110° to 120°F)
1½ teaspoons granulated sugar
2¾ cups sifted all-purpose flour

1 teaspoon salt
¼ cup yellow cornmeal
2 tablespoons salad oil

Grease a large glass bowl and set aside. In a large, glass measuring cup, dissolve yeast in warm water. Add sugar to yeast and let stand for 5 minutes. Place steel cutting blade into container. Add flour and salt. While food processor is running, pour yeast mixture down feed tube. Process just until dough forms a ball, about 10 to 15 seconds. Remove dough ball from container and roll in greased bowl, until dough ball is well greased. Cover and let rise 90 minutes. Punch down, remove from bowl, and let rest on a lightly floured board for 10 minutes. Dust an ungreased cookie sheet with cornmeal. Form dough into long loaf and place on cookie sheet. Cover and allow to rise 90 minutes. Preheat oven to 375°F and place a shallow pan of water in bottom of oven. Before baking, brush loaf lightly with salad oil. Bake for 40 to 50 minutes.

BISCUITS   Yield: 8 2" biscuits

These baking powder biscuits can be brought to the table for breakfast, lunch and dinner — hot, light and fresh from the oven.

2 cups sifted all-purpose flour
1 tablespoon baking powder
½ teaspoon salt

¼ cup butter or margarine, melted
¾ cup milk

Preheat oven to 450°F. Place steel cutting blade into container. Sift flour, baking powder, and salt into container. Add melted butter to milk. While processor is running, pour butter mixture down feed tube. Process just until a dough ball forms. DO NOT OVERPROCESS. Place dough onto a lightly floured board. Cover with waxed paper. Roll to ½" thickness. Cut into rounds with biscuit cutter. Place on ungreased baking sheetw Bake for 12 to 15 minutes. Serve warm.

CORNBREAD   Yield: Serves 6 to 8

Especially good with fried chicken. It can also be made into tiny sandwiches with pieces of ham to be served as hors d'oeuvres.

1 cup sifted all-purpose flour
¼ cup granulated sugar
4 teaspoons baking powder
¾ teaspoon salt

1 cup cornmeal
2 eggs
¼ cup melted butter or margarine
1 cup milk

Preheat oven to 425°F. Grease a 9" x 9" x 2" baking pan. Place steel cutting blade into container. Sift flour, sugar, baking powder, and salt into container. Add cornmeal and eggs. Add melted butter to milk. While processor is running, pour milk mixture down feed tube. Process until mixture is blended. DO NOT OVERPROCESS. Pour batter into prepared pan. Bake for 20 to 25 minutes. Remove from oven. While still warm, cut into pieces and serve.

Variation: CORNSTICKS   Yield: 21 cornsticks
Prepare batter as directed above. Pour into well-greased, heated cornstick pans and bake for 15 to 20 minutes in a 425°F oven.

PUMPKIN BREAD   Yield: 1 loaf

A flavorful bread with cinnamon, nutmeg, and all-spice to combine with the pumpkin.

1 cup granulated sugar
½ cup salad oil
2 eggs, beaten
1 cup cooked, mashed pumpkin
1¾ cups sifted all-purpose flour
½ teaspoon baking powder
1 teaspoon baking soda

1 teaspoon salt
¼ teaspoon ground cloves
½ teaspoon ground cinnamon
½ teaspoon ground nutmeg
½ teaspoon ground allspice
¼ cup water

Preheat oven to 350°F. Grease a 9" x 5" x 3" loaf pan. Place steel cutting blade into container. Add sugar, salad oil, eggs, and pumpkin and process until smooth. Remove cover and scrape down container sides. Sift flour, baking powder, baking soda, salt, cloves, cinnamon, nutmeg, and allspice into container. Process, adding water through the feed tube, until well blended. Pour into prepared loaf pan. Bake for 60 to 80 minutes, or until a toothpick inserted into center of loaf comes out clean. Remove from pan and cool on wire rack.

RAISIN-APPLESAUCE LOAF   Yield: 1 loaf

This is an unfrosted cake that you might serve with whipped cream.

1 cup shelled walnut halves
½ cup granulated sugar
¼ cup brown sugar
1 egg
1 cup applesauce
¼ cup butter or margarine,
   cut into 4 pieces

2 cups sifted all-purpose flour
2 teaspoons baking powder
½ teaspoon baking soda
½ teaspoon salt
½ teaspoon cinnamon
½ teaspoon nutmeg
½ cup raisins

Preheat oven to 350°F. Grease a 9" x 5" x 3" loaf pan. Place steel cutting blade into container. Chop walnuts. Empty chopped nuts onto waxed paper. Place steel cutting blade into container. Process sugars, egg, applesauce, and butter until creamy. Remove cover and scrape down container sides. Sift flour, baking powder, baking soda, salt, cinnamon, and nutmeg into container. Process until well blended. Remove cover and scrape down container sides. Add raisins and walnuts. Process until combined. Pour into prepared pan. Bake for 60 to 75 minutes, or until toothpick inserted into center of loaf comes out clean. Remove loaf from pan and cool on a wire rack.

BANANA-NUT BREAD   Yield: 1 loaf

Moist and tender, this bread makes a wonderful tea bread.

½ cup butter or margarine, softened
1 cup brown sugar, firmly packed
2 eggs
2 bananas, cut into 1" pieces
2 cups sifted all-purpose flour

½ teaspoon salt
½ teaspoon baking soda
⅓ cup buttermilk
½ cup shelled chopped walnuts

Preheat oven to 350°F. Grease a 9" x 5" x 3" loaf pan. Place steel cutting blade into container. Add butter and brown sugar. Process until creamy. Remove cover and scrape down container sides. Add eggs and bananas and process until well blended. Remove cover and scrape down container sides. Sift flour, salt, and baking soda into container. Process while slowly pouring buttermilk through feed tube. Remove cover and add chopped nuts. Process until nuts are evenly distributed throughout batter. Pour into prepared pan. Bake for 60 to 80 minutes, or until a toothpick inserted into center of loaf comes out clean. Remove from pan and cool on wire rack.

BASIC MUFFIN BATTER   Yield: 1 dozen muffins

1¾ cups sifted all-purpose flour
¼ cup granulated sugar
2½ teaspoons baking powder
½ teaspoon salt

1 egg
¾ cup milk
½ cup salad oil

Preheat oven to 400°F. Grease 12 muffin cups. Place steel cutting blade into container. Sift flour, sugar, baking powder, and salt into container. Add egg. Use TOUCH-ON control to mix ingredients together. Remove cover and scrape down container sides. While processor is running, pour milk and vegetable oil down feed tube. Process until mixture is well blended. DO NOT OVER-PROCESS. Fill prepared muffin cups about ⅔ full. Bake 15 to 20 minutes. Serve warm.

Variations:
Blueberry Muffins: Prepare batter as directed above. Add 1 cup fresh blueberries after batter is processed.

Date Muffins: Prepare batter as directed above. Add ¾ cup coarsely chopped dates after batter is processed.

Raisin Muffins: Prepare batter as directed above. Add ½ cup raisins after batter is processed.

TROPICAL FRUIT MUFFINS   Yield: 1 dozen

A change from the ordinary muffins, these have banana, orange juice, and pineapple added.

½ cup shelled pecans
1 large banana, cut into 1" pieces
½ cup orange juice
½ cup (4 ounces) crushed pineapple
¼ cup butter or margarine, softened,
  and cut into 1" pieces

½ cup granulated sugar
1 egg
1 cup sifted all-purpose flour
1 teaspoon baking powder
½ teaspoon baking soda
¼ teaspoon salt

Preheat oven to 350°F. Line muffin cups with paper liners. Place steel cutting blade into container. Coarsely chop nuts. Empty onto waxed paper. Place steel cutting blade into container. Purée banana slices. Pour into a small mixing bowl. Add orange juice and pineapple to puréed banana. Stir to mix. Set aside. Place steel cutting blade into container. Add butter and sugar. Process until light and fluffy. Add egg and process until well blended. Remove cover and scrape down container sides. Sift flour, baking powder, baking soda, and salt into container. Process, using TOUCH-ON control, until blended. Remove cover. Pour banana mixture into container. Process only until blended. Sprinkle chopped nuts over batter. Process, using TOUCH-ON control, until blended, about 2 to 3 seconds. Spoon batter into muffin cups until ⅔ full. Bake for 35 to 40 minutes, or until golden brown. Serve warm.

PROCESSOR POPOVERS   Yield: 1 dozen

Serve with butter and honey or maple syrup. Popovers may also be used as cups for salads and creamed food.

2 eggs
1 cup milk
1 tablespoon butter or margarine, melted

1 cup sifted all-purpose flour
½ teaspoon salt

Preheat oven to 425°F. Grease 12 muffin cups. Place steel cutting blade into container. Add eggs and process until foamy. Add milk and butter. Process until blended. Remove cover and add flour and salt. Process until blended. Fill muffin cups half full. Bake 40 to 50 minutes. Prick each popover using a knife and bake 10 minutes longer. Remove from muffin cups and serve immediately.

SUGARY SPICE PUFFS   Yield: 3 dozen

Sugar-coated, ginger muffins.

¼ cup butter or margarine, softened
1¼ cups granulated sugar, divided
1 egg
1 cup milk
2 teaspoons grated lemon rind
2 cups sifted all-purpose flour

4 teaspoons baking powder
½ teaspoon salt
¼ teaspoon nutmeg
2 teaspoons ginger
¼ cup butter or margarine, melted

Preheat oven to 375°F. Grease muffin cups. Place steel cutting blade into container. Add butter and ½ cup sugar. Process until creamy. Add egg, milk, and lemon peel. Process until thoroughly combined. Remove cover. Sift flour, baking powder, salt, and nutmeg into container. Process only until combined. Spoon into prepared muffin cups until half full. Bake 15 minutes. Mix ginger with remaining sugar. While muffins are hot, dip each into melted butter, then roll in sugar mixture. Serve warm or cool.

LEMON TEA BREAD   Yield: 1 loaf

A light bread raised by baking powder and served cold.

BREAD

1½ cups sifted all-purpose flour
½ teaspoon salt
1 teaspoon baking powder
1¼ cups granulated sugar

½ cup butter or margarine, melted
2 eggs
Juice of 1 lemon
Grated rind of 1 lemon

Preheat oven to 350°F. Grease a 9″ x 5″ x 3″ loaf pan. Place steel cutting blade into container. Sift flour, salt, baking powder, and sugar into container. Process, using TOUCH-ON control, until ingredients are mixed. Remove cover. Add butter, eggs, lemon juice, and lemon rind. Process until batter is smooth. Pour into prepared loaf pan. Bake for 1 hour or until toothpick inserted into center of loaf comes out clean. Remove from pan.

GLAZE

½ cup confectioners sugar
Juice of 1 lemon

Grated rind of 1 lemon

Combine all ingredients in a small bowl. Spread over warm loaf. Chill for 4 hours before serving.

DOUGHNUT PUFFS Yield: 2½ dozen

Dainty deep-fried delicate tidbits.

2 tablespoons butter or margarine
½ cup granulated sugar
2 eggs
½ cup milk
2 cups sifted all-purpose flour
2 teaspoons baking powder

½ teaspoon salt
½ teaspoon mace
¼ teaspoon nutmeg
Oil for frying
2 teaspoons cinnamon
½ cup sugar

Place steel cutting blade into container. Add butter and sugar. Process until creamy. Add eggs and milk. Process until thoroughly combined. Remove cover. Sift flour, baking powder, salt, mace, and nutmeg into container. Process until a smooth, soft dough is formed. Transfer to small mixing bowl. Chill dough thoroughly. Heat oil to desired temperature in a deep fryer. Drop dough by rounded teaspoonfuls into hot oil, dipping spoon into hot oil each time before putting into batter (do not overcrowd). Fry until golden brown, turning to brown evenly, about 2 to 3 minutes. Remove puffs with slotted spoon. Drain on paper towels. Mix cinnamon and sugar in a small mixing bowl. Roll puffs in cinnamon and sugar mixture while still warm. Repeat with remaining dough.

EASY PIE FILLING COFFEECAKE Yield: Serves 10 to 12

A rich coffeecake, quickly done.

¾ cup butter or margarine
1 cup granulated sugar
3 eggs
2 tablespoons milk
½ teaspoon vanilla extract
2 cups sifted cake flour

1 teaspoon baking powder
½ teaspoon salt
1 (21-ounce) can favorite prepared
   pie filling flavor
Confectioners sugar

Preheat oven to 400°F. Grease and dust with flour a 13" x 9" x 2" baking pan. Place steel cutting blade into container. Add butter and sugar. Process until creamy. Add eggs, milk, and vanilla extract. Process until well blended, about 1 minute. Remove cover and scrape down container sides. Sift flour, baking powder, and salt into container. Process until batter is smooth and well blended. Pour ¾ of the batter into prepared pan. Top with pie filling. Drizzle the remaining batter over the pie filling. Bake for 15 minutes, then reduce heat to 350°F and continue baking for 30 to 35 minutes, until golden brown. Cool for 10 minutes in pan on wire rack. Sprinkle with confectioners sugar and serve.

Variation: Drizzle with Confectioners Glaze (see page 108).

BANANA-CHEESE COFFEECAKE   Yield: Serves 4 to 6

A luscious coffeecake with a nutty topping. The steel blade does it all.

CAKE

1½ cups sifted all-purpose flour
½ cup granulated sugar
2 teaspoons baking powder
½ teaspoon salt
1 egg

1 (3-ounce) package cream cheese,
  cut into chunks
1 banana, cut into 5 pieces
¼ cup milk

Preheat oven to 350°F. Grease a 9" x 9" x 2" square baking pan. Place steel cutting blade into container. Sift flour, sugar, baking powder, and salt into container. Add egg, cream cheese, and banana. While processor is running, pour milk down feed tube. Process until batter is smooth. Pour batter into prepared baking pan.

TOPPING

1 cup shelled pecans
2 tablespoons brown sugar

1 teaspoon cinnamon

Place steel cutting blade into container. Add pecans, brown sugar, and cinnamon. Process until pecans are coarsely chopped. Swirl half of the pecan mixture into batter. Sprinkle the other half of the mixture over top of batter. Bake for 35 to 40 minutes. Serve warm.

APPLE CRUMB CAKE   Yield: Serves 6 to 8

The food processor makes this cake so easy to prepare, you'll want to make it often.

CAKE

4 medium apples, cored, peeled,
  and quartered
1½ cups sifted all-purpose flour
½ cup granulated sugar
2 teaspoons baking powder

½ teaspoon salt
½ cup milk
1 egg
¼ cup salad oil

Preheat oven to 350°F. Grease an 8" x 8" x 2" baking pan. Place slicing disc into container. Slice apples. Empty sliced apples onto waxed paper. Place steel cutting blade into container. Sift flour, sugar, baking powder, and salt into container. Add milk, egg, and oil. Process until batter is smooth. Pour mixture into prepared pan. Place apple slices over batter.

TOPPING

¼ cup sifted all-purpose flour
⅔ cup brown sugar, firmly packed

2 tablespoons butter or margarine, melted
1 teaspoon cinnamon

Place steel cutting blade into container. Add all ingredients to container. Process until moistened. Sprinkle topping over cake mixture. Bake for 35 to 40 minutes. Serve warm.

CARAMEL PECAN ROLLS   Yield: 16 rolls

These sweet and sticky rolls have been a favored breakfast or brunch treat for a long time. They should be prepared a day ahead and refrigerated before baking.

SWEET DOUGH

¼ cup granulated sugar
1 package active dry yeast
½ cup milk (120° to 130°F)
3¼ cups sifted all-purpose flour, divided

1 teaspoon salt
⅔ cup butter or margarine, softened,
  cut into pieces
2 eggs

In a glass measuring cup, dissolve sugar and yeast in warm milk. Allow to rest for 5 minutes. Meanwhile, place steel cutting blade into container. Add 3 cups flour, salt, and butter to container. Process, using TOUCH-ON control, 5 times. Add eggs and process until mixture is crumbly. Pour yeast mixture through feed tube and process 5 to 10 seconds, or until mixture is well blended. Turn unit OFF and allow to rest for 2 minutes. Add ¼ cup flour and process just until dough ball is formed. Remove cover and scrape sides of container. Place dough ball in a large, greased bowl.

TOPPING AND FILLING

¾ cup shelled pecans
1 cup brown sugar, firmly packed
½ cup butter or margarine, melted
3 tablespoons water

3 tablespoons butter or margarine,
  softened
½ cup granulated sugar
1 teaspoon cinnamon

Grease a 13" x 9" x 2" baking pan. Place steel cutting blade into container. Add pecans and coarsely chop. Empty chopped pecans onto a sheet of waxed paper. Place steel cutting blade into container. Add brown sugar, melted butter, and water. Process until smooth. Spread brown sugar mixture over bottom of prepared pan. Arrange pecans on top of brown sugar mixture in pan. Roll dough into a 16" x 10" rectangle. Spread the rectangle with the softened butter. Combine the sugar and cinnamon and sprinkle onto dough. Roll up like a jelly roll, beginning with the long side. Seal edges. Cut into 16 slices 1" each. Place rolls cut side down, on top of pecans, spacing the rolls 2" apart. Cover and refrigerate for 2 to 24 hours. Preheat oven to 425°F. Bake for 15 to 20 minutes. Invert pan onto waxed paper. Let stand for 5 to 10 minutes to allow caramel mixture to coat rolls. Serve warm.

CHOCOLATE CHEESECAKE   Yield: Serves 4 to 6

This cake is so rich, good and easy, it's perfect for busy modern people who like to entertain.

1 baked graham cracker crust prepared in
  an 8" x 8" x 2" baking pan (see page 105)
½ cup granulated sugar
2 eggs
1 (8-ounce) package cream cheese,
  cut into chunks

1 (6-ounce) package semi-sweet chocolate
  chips, melted
½ cup sour cream
½ teaspoon vanilla extract
Whipped topping (optional)

Preheat oven to 350°F. Place steel cutting blade into container. Add sugar, eggs, and cream cheese. Process until smooth. Remove cover and scrape down container sides. Add remaining ingredients and process until well blended. Pour into prepared crust. Bake for 30 to 35 minutes, or until center is firm. Cool on wire rack. Refrigerate overnight. Serve chilled with whipped topping, if desired.

CARROT CAKE   Yield: Serves 9 to 12

This is a light, nutty flavored cake. Sometimes currants and raisins are added with the nuts.

4 to 5 medium carrots, peeled
1 cup granulated sugar
½ cup vegetable oil
2 eggs
¼ cup water
1 teaspoon baking powder
1 teaspoon baking soda

1 teaspoon cinnamon
½ teaspoon salt
⅛ teaspoon ginger
⅛ teaspoon nutmeg
½ teaspoon vanilla extract
1½ cups sifted all-purpose flour
½ cup shelled walnuts

Preheat oven to 375°F. Grease and dust with flour a 9" x 9" x 2" square baking pan. Place shredding disc into container. Shred carrots. Empty onto a sheet of waxed paper. Place steel cutting blade into container. Add sugar, oil, eggs, water, baking powder, baking soda, cinnamon, salt, ginger, nutmeg, vanilla extract, and shredded carrots. Process until well blended. Add flour. Process until combined. Add walnuts. Process, using TOUCH-ON control, until blended. Turn into prepared baking pan. Bake 30 to 35 minutes, or until toothpick inserted into center of cake comes out clean. Cool cake in pan for 5 minutes. Loosen edges of cake with spatula and turn onto wire rack. Cool completely before frosting.

Suggested Frosting: Cream Cheese Frosting (see page 108).

ITALIAN CHEESECAKE   Yield: Serves 10 to 12

Here is a large cheesecake to serve a crowd. It must be refrigerated overnight.

CRUST

1¼ cups sifted all-purpose flour
¼ cup granulated sugar
½ teaspoon salt
½ teaspoon grated lemon peel

½ cup softened butter or margarine,
   cut into 6 pieces
1 egg yolk, beaten
2 tablespoons Galliano liqueur

Preheat oven to 350°F. Place steel cutting blade into container. Add flour, sugar, salt, lemon peel, and butter. Process until mixture resembles coarse crumbs. In a measuring cup, mix egg yolk and Galliano together. While processor is running, pour egg yolk mixture down feed tube. Process until all ingredients are well blended. Press crust mixture over bottom of an ungreased 9″ springform pan. Bake for 10 to 15 minutes until dry, but not browned.

FILLING

2 (15-ounce) containers Ricotta cheese
4 eggs
½ cup granulated sugar
¼ cup sifted all-purpose flour

¼ cup Galliano liqueur
1 teaspoon lemon peel
1 tablespoon lemon juice

Place steel cutting blade into container. Add Ricotta cheese, eggs, sugar, and flour. Process until blended. Remove cover and add Galliano, lemon peel, and lemon juice. Process until smooth. Pour filling over warm crust and bake for 1 hour. Turn off heat. Let cheesecake stand in oven for 1 hour. Remove from oven and cool on wire rack. Refrigerate overnight. Before serving, remove springform rim. Cut into wedges.

CHOCOLATE NUT TORTE   Yield: Serves 8 to 10

CAKE

3 (1-ounce) squares unsweetened chocolate
2 cups sifted cake flour
1 teaspoon baking soda
1 teaspoon salt
⅓ cup butter or margarine, softened

1 cup sour cream
1½ cups granulated sugar
2 eggs
1 teaspoon almond extract
¼ cup hot water (110° to 120°F)

Preheat oven to 350°F. Grease and dust with flour three 8″ cake pans. Melt chocolate in a double boiler. Cool. Place steel cutting blade into container. Sift flour, baking soda, and salt into container. Add butter, sour cream, and sugar. Process, while slowly pouring eggs, almond extract, cooled chocolate, and hot water down feed tube. Scrape down container sides, as necessary. Continue processing until well blended. Divide batter into 3 parts and pour into prepared pans. Bake for 30 to 35 minutes, or until a toothpick inserted into center of cake comes out clean. Cool cake in pans for 5 minutes. Loosen edges of cake with a spatula and turn onto wire racks. Cool completely before frosting.

NUT FILLING

¾ cup granulated sugar
¾ cup evaporated milk
3 egg yolks
½ cup butter or margarine

1 teaspoon vanilla extract
1 (3½-ounce) can flaked coconut (1½ cups)
1 cup shelled chopped walnuts

Combine sugar, evaporated milk, egg yolks, butter, and vanilla extract in saucepan. Cook over medium heat, stirring constantly until thickened. Remove from heat. Stir in coconut and walnuts. Cool. Spread filling onto bottom layer; top with second layer. Repeat with remaining filling and layer. Spread remaining filling over top of cake. Cover cake and chill before serving.

CHEESECAKE Yield: Serves 8 to 10

Rich and creamy; a perennial favorite dessert.

1 unbaked 9″ x 9″ x 2″ graham cracker
   crust (see page 105)
3 (8-ounce) packages cream cheese,
   softened, and cut into chunks
Juice of 1 lemon

1 cup granulated sugar
2 tablespoons sifted all-purpose flour
3 eggs
¼ cup light cream

Preheat oven to 450°F. Place steel cutting blade into container. Add cream cheese. Pour lemon juice over cheese. Process, while slowly adding sugar and flour through feed tube. Add eggs and process until smooth. Add cream and process until blended. Pour into prepared graham cracker crust. Bake for 15 minutes, then reduce heat to 200°F and bake for 1 hour. Turn oven off and allow cheesecake to remain in oven for 10 minutes. Chill thoroughly before serving.

Serving Suggestion: Top with whipped cream or fruit pie filling.

LEMON BARS   Yield: 16 cookies

Perfect cookies to serve with fruit salad.

CRUST

½ cup butter or margarine,
   cut into 6 pieces

1¼ cups sifted all-purpose flour
¼ cup confectioners sugar

Preheat oven to 350°F. Place steel cutting blade into container. Add butter, flour, and confectioners sugar. Process until mixture has a crumbly texture. Press into an ungreased 8″ x 8″ x 2″ baking pan, forming a raised edge. Bake for 15 to 20 minutes, or until lightly browned.

LEMON FILLING

¾ cup granulated sugar
2 eggs
1 tablespoon sifted all-purpose flour

¼ teaspoon baking powder
¼ cup freshly squeezed lemon juice
2 teaspoons grated lemon rind

While crust is baking, prepare the lemon filling. Place steel cutting blade into container. Add sugar, eggs, flour, baking powder, lemon juice, and rind. Process until well blended. Remove cover and scrape down container sides. Pour filling over partially baked crust and bake for an additional 15 to 20 minutes. Cool in pan on wire rack. Cut into 2″ squares.

Serving Suggestion: Sprinkle with confectioners sugar.

PEANUT BUTTER COOKIES   Yield: 2 dozen 2" cookies

A traditional after school treat. Take care not to chop the peanuts too fine, or you'll lose the doubly peanutty effect.

½ cup cocktail-style salted peanuts
½ cup shortening
½ cup creamy-style peanut butter
½ cup brown sugar, firmly packed
¼ cup granulated sugar

1 egg
1¼ cups sifted all-purpose flour
1 teaspoon baking soda
¼ teaspoon salt
½ teaspoon vanilla extract

Preheat oven to 350°F. Place steel cutting blade into container. Chop peanuts. Empty chopped peanuts onto waxed paper. Place steel cutting blade into container. Add shortening, peanut butter, and sugars. Process until smooth and creamy. Add egg and process until well blended. Remove cover and scrape down container sides. Sift flour, baking soda, and salt into container. Process until well blended. Add vanilla extract and chopped peanuts and process until thoroughly combined. Roll mixture into 1" balls. Place on ungreased cookie sheet. Flatten with fork to form crisscross pattern. Bake for 10 to 12 minutes, or until edges are golden brown. Cool on wire racks.

BROWNIES   Yield: 16 squares

Cream cheese gives these brownies a slightly different flavor.

½ cup shelled walnuts
¼ cup butter or margarine,
    cut into pieces
3 ounces cream cheese, cut into chunks
2 eggs
½ teaspoon vanilla extract

¾ cup sifted all-purpose flour
¼ cup cocoa
¼ teaspoon baking powder
¼ teaspoon salt
1 cup granulated sugar

Preheat oven to 350°F. Grease an 8" x 8" x 2" baking pan. Place steel cutting blade into container. Coarsely chop walnuts. Empty onto waxed paper. Place steel cutting blade into container. Add butter, cream cheese, eggs, and vanilla extract. Process until smooth. Remove cover and scrape down container sides. Sift flour, cocoa, baking powder, salt, and sugar into container. Process until ingredients are well blended. Stir walnuts into batter. Pour batter into prepared pan. Bake for 30 to 35 minutes. Spread with desired frosting while still warm. Cool and cut into 2" squares.

ALMOND MACAROONS   Yield: 5 to 6 dozen cookies

Light and lovely little cookies. Keep these in mind to serve with a fruit or ice cream dessert.

1 (8-ounce) can almond paste,   1 cup granulated sugar
   divided into chunks   2 egg whites

Preheat oven to 300°F. Grease a cookie sheet. Place steel cutting blade into container. Add almond paste. Process until mixture has a crumbly texture. Add sugar. Process until well blended, about 15 seconds. While processing, pour egg whites down feed tube. Continue processing just until dough ball forms. DO NOT OVERPROCESS. Drop by teaspoonfuls onto prepared cookie sheet. Bake for 30 to 35 minutes, until golden brown. Remove from pan and cool on wire racks.

Hint: If dough ball does not form or is very sticky, add 1 to 2 additional tablespoons granulated sugar.

BUTTERSCOTCH REFRIGERATOR COOKIES   Yield: 3 dozen

This recipe puts the steel blade to work chopping pecans and mixing the dough. Your cookies are crisp and good eating.

2 ounces shelled pecan halves   2 cups sifted all-purpose flour
½ cup butter or margarine, softened   1 teaspoon baking powder
1 cup brown sugar, firmly packed   ⅛ teaspoon baking soda
1 egg   ¼ teaspoon salt
1 teaspoon vanilla extract

Preheat oven to 375°F. Place steel cutting blade into container. Chop pecan halves. Empty onto waxed paper. Place steel cutting blade into container. Add butter, brown sugar, egg, and vanilla extract. Process until creamy, about 30 seconds. Remove cover and sift flour, baking powder, baking soda, and salt into container. Process until a dough ball forms. Place dough into a large bowl. Stir in chopped pecans. Form dough into 2 rolls 2" in diameter. Wrap in waxed paper. Refrigerate 1 hour. Slice cookie dough into ¼"-thick slices. Place on ungreased cookie sheet and bake 10 to 12 minutes, or until lightly browned. Cool on wire racks.

SUGAR COOKIES   Yield: 4 to 5 dozen 2" cookies

A standard cookie jar item that your food processor can help you produce with ease.

½ cup butter or margarine, softened
1½ cups granulated sugar, divided
1 egg
½ teaspoon vanilla extract
¼ teaspoon lemon extract
2 cups sifted all-purpose flour

1 teaspoon baking powder
¼ teaspoon baking soda
¼ teaspoon salt
¼ teaspoon nutmeg
¼ cup milk
1 egg white, beaten

Preheat oven to 375°F. Place steel cutting blade into container. Add butter, 1 cup sugar, egg, vanilla extract, and lemon extract. Process until smooth. Remove cover and scrape down container sides. Sift flour, baking powder, baking soda, salt, and nutmeg into container. Process, while gradually adding milk through feed tube, until dough forms a ball. Refrigerate dough until easy to handle. Meanwhile, grease a cookie sheet. Roll mixture into 1" balls. Place onto prepared cookie sheet. Dip bottom of glass into beaten egg white and then into remaining ½ cup sugar. Flatten dough ball to ¼" with bottom of glass. Repeat procedure for each dough ball. Bake for 8 to 10 minutes, or until edges become light brown. Remove from cookie sheet and cool on wire racks. Repeat for remaining cookie dough.

FUDGE DROPS   Yield: 4 to 5 dozen 2" cookies

Long enduring first choice chocolate cookies.

2 (1-ounce) squares unsweetened
  chocolate
⅔ cup shortening
1 cup brown sugar, firmly packed
1 egg
1¾ cups sifted all-purpose flour

½ teaspoon baking soda
½ teaspoon salt
½ cup milk
1 teaspoon vanilla extract
1 cup chopped nuts

Preheat oven to 350°F. Grease a cookie sheet. Melt chocolate in a double boiler. Set aside to cool. Place steel cutting blade into container. Add shortening, brown sugar, egg, and cooled chocolate. Process until well blended. Remove cover and scrape down container sides. Sift flour, baking soda, and salt into container. Add milk and vanilla extract. Process until smooth. Add chopped nuts and process until just combined. Drop by rounded teaspoonfuls onto prepared cookie sheet. Bake for 8 to 10 minutes, or until edges are golden brown. Cool on wire racks. Repeat for remaining cookie dough.

Suggested Frosting: Mocha Frosting (see page 108).

LEMONY DROP COOKIES   Yield: 5 dozen

An attractive contrast to the chocolate cookies on your holiday tray, these are as good as they look.

¼ cup lemon juice
1 tablespoon grated lemon rind
¼ cup water
½ cup butter, softened
1 egg

1 cup granulated sugar
½ teaspoon salt
2 cups sifted all-purpose flour
1 tablespoon baking powder

Preheat oven to 400°F. Grease a cookie sheet. Place steel cutting blade into container. Add lemon juice, lemon rind, water, butter, egg, sugar, and salt. Process until smooth. Remove cover and scrape down container sides. Sift flour and baking powder into container. Process until well mixed. Drop by level tablespoonfuls onto prepared cookie sheet. Bake at 400°F for 8 minutes, or until bottom of cookie is lightly browned. Remove cookies and cool on wire racks. Repeat for remaining dough.

Suggested Frosting: Frost cookies with Fresh Lemon Frosting (see page 109).

SPRITZ COOKIES   Yield: 5 dozen 2″ cookies

These fancily shaped cookies are made by pressing the dough through a cookie press.

1 cup butter, softened and cut into pieces
¾ cup brown sugar, firmly packed
1 egg yolk
2 cups sifted all-purpose flour

¼ teaspoon salt
½ teaspoon vanilla extract
colored sugar (optional)

Preheat oven to 350°F. Place steel cutting blade into container. Add butter, brown sugar, and egg yolk. Process until light and fluffy. Remove cover and scrape down container sides. Add flour, salt, and vanilla extract. Process until well blended. Press dough through a cookie press onto an ungreased cookie sheet. Decorate, if desired, with colored sugar. Bake for 8 to 10 minutes, or until lightly browned. Cool on wire racks.

APPLE CRISP   Yield: Serves 6 to 8

6 large apples, cored and halved
⅔ cup brown sugar, firmly packed
½ cup sifted all-purpose flour
¾ teaspoon cinnamon

¾ teaspoon nutmeg
7 tablespoons chilled butter
½ cup rolled oats

Preheat oven to 375°F. Grease an 8″ x 8″ x 2″ pan. Place slicing disc into container. Slice apples. Empty into greased pan. Place steel cutting blade into container. Add brown sugar. Process, using TOUCH-ON control, 2 times. Add remaining ingredients. Process, using TOUCH-ON control, until crumbly. Sprinkle over apples. Bake for 25 to 35 minutes, or until apples are tender and topping is golden brown. Serve warm.

PUMPKIN PIE   Yield: Serves 8 to 10

1 unbaked, 10" deep-dish pastry shell,
   chilled (see page 104)
3 eggs
1½ cups cooked or canned pumpkin
½ cup brown sugar, firmly packed
½ teaspoon salt

1½ teaspoons cinnamon
½ teaspoon ginger
½ teaspoon nutmeg
1 teaspoon vanilla extract
1 (13-ounce) can evaporated milk
Whipped topping (optional)

Preheat oven to 450°F. Place steel cutting blade into container. Add eggs and process for 20 seconds. Remove cover and scrape down container sides. Add remaining ingredients and process until well blended. Pour mixture into prepared pastry shell. Bake for 15 minutes then reduce temperature to 350°F. Bake for 45 to 60 minutes, or until a knife inserted into center of pie comes out clean. Serve slightly warm with whipped topping, if desired.

SOUR CREAM PIE   Yield: Serves 4 to 6

1 unbaked 9" pastry shell (see page 104)
2 eggs
1 cup sour cream
½ cup granulated sugar

1 teaspoon cinnamon
¼ teaspoon salt
½ cup shelled pecan halves
1 cup seedless raisins

Preheat oven to 450°F. Place steel cutting blade into container. Add eggs, sour cream, sugar, cinnamon, and salt. Process until mixture is well blended. Remove cover and scrape down container sides. Add pecans and raisins. Process until thoroughly combined. Pour mixture into prepared pastry shell. Bake for 15 minutes then lower oven temperature to 350°F and bake for 45 to 60 minutes, or until a knife inserted into center of pie comes out clean. Cool to room temperature before serving.

APPLE PIE WITH CRUMB TOPPING   Yield: Serves 6 to 8

PIE

1 unbaked 9" pastry shell (see below)
6 apples, cored, peeled, and quartered
¼ cup granulated sugar
½ cup brown sugar

3 tablespoons sifted all-purpose flour
½ teaspoon nutmeg
¾ teaspoon cinnamon
2 tablespoons butter or margarine, melted

Preheat oven to 425°F. Place slicing disc into container. Slice apples. Empty apples into a large bowl. Place steel cutting blade into container. Add granulated and brown sugars, flour, nutmeg, and cinnamon. While processor is running, pour butter down feed tube. Process until mixture is moistened. Add to apples. Stir to blend. Pour into prepared pastry shell. Cover with Crumb Topping.

CRUMB TOPPING

1 cup sifted all-purpose flour
¼ cup granulated sugar
½ cup brown sugar

½ teaspoon cinnamon
½ cup butter or margarine, melted

Place steel cutting blade into container. Add flour, granulated and brown sugars, and cinnamon. While processor is running, pour butter down feed tube. Process until topping is moistened. Sprinkle over the apple mixture. Bake for 40 to 50 minutes or until topping is golden brown. Serve warm.

PASTRY SHELL   Yield: An 8", 9", or 10" single-crust pie shell

1½ cups sifted all-purpose flour
½ cup shortening
½ teaspoon salt

1 teaspoon baking powder
5 to 6 tablespoons cold water

Preheat oven to 450°F. Place steel cutting blade into container. Add flour, shortening, salt, and baking powder. Process until fine crumbs are formed. Process, while pouring water through feed tube, a little at a time, until dough ball forms. Flatten onto a lightly-floured board. Roll to ⅛" thickness. Fit pastry to desired-size pie pan. Trim edge, turn under, and flute. Prick bottom and sides with a fork. *Do not prick shell if it is to be filled before baking.* Bake for 10 to 12 minutes, or until golden brown. Cool.

Variation: To make tart shells, roll to ⅛" thickness. Cut into 5" or 6" circles. Fit into tart pans. Press out bubbles. Trim edge, turn under, and flute. Bake as directed above.

CRUMB CRUSTS

GRAHAM CRACKER

SIZE	CRUMB AMOUNT	GRANULATED SUGAR	BUTTER OR MARGARINE
8″	1¼ cups (16 2″ squares)	1 tablespoon	¼ cup, melted
9″	1½ cups (21 2″ squares)	1 tablespoon	¼ cup, melted
10″	1¾ cups (26 2″ squares)	1 tablespoon	5 tablespoons, melted

VANILLA WAFER

SIZE	CRUMB AMOUNT	GRANULATED SUGAR	BUTTER OR MARGARINE
8″	1¼ cups (33 wafers)	1 tablespoon	¼ cup, melted
9″	1½ cups (40 wafers)	1 tablespoon	¼ cup, melted
10″	1¾ cups (54 wafers)	1 tablespoon	¼ cup, melted

CHOCOLATE WAFER

SIZE	CRUMB AMOUNT	GRANULATED SUGAR	BUTTER OR MARGARINE
8″	1¼ cups (24 wafers)	2 tablespoons	¼ cup, melted
9″	1½ cups (29 wafers)	2 tablespoons	¼ cup, melted
10″	1¾ cups (38 wafers)	2 tablespoons	5 tablespoons, melted

Preheat oven to 350°F. Place steel cutting blade into container. While processor is running, drop crackers or wafers down feed tube. Run processor until crumbs are formed. Remove cover. Add sugar. While processor is running, pour butter down feed tube. Process until mixture is moistened. Press mixture into pan. Bake for 10 minutes. Cool before adding filling.

PÂTE BRISÉE   Yield: 1 10" pastry shell

1¾ cups sifted all-purpose flour
¾ cup butter, cut into 6 pieces

1 large egg, lightly beaten
Dash of salt

Preheat oven to 425°F. Place steel cutting blade into container. Distribute each ingredient evenly over bottom of container. Process for 10 seconds. Remove the dough and form into a ball with your hands. Place onto a sheet of waxed paper. Pat dough into an 11" circle. Invert into an ungreased 10" deep-dish pie or quiche pan. Peel off waxed paper. Pat evenly over bottom and sides of pan. Bake for 10 minutes until dry but not browned.

FRENCH SILK PIE   Yield: Serves 6 to 8

½ cup butter, softened
¾ cup confectioners sugar
1 (1-ounce) square unsweetened chocolate,
   melted and cooled
1 teaspoon vanilla extract

2 eggs
1 baked 9" pastry shell (see page 104)
Whipped cream (optional)
Shaved chocolate (optional)

Place steel cutting blade into container. Cream butter. Remove lid. Add confectioners sugar and blend until mixture becomes light and fluffy. Scrape down container sides, as necessary. Add chocolate, vanilla extract, and 1 egg. Process for 2 minutes. Scrape down container sides. Add second egg. Process 2 minutes longer. Pour into prepared pastry shell. Chill for 2 hours. Garnish with whipped cream and shaved chocolate, if desired.

Variation: For 8 individual servings, spoon chilled French Silk mixture onto dessert crêpes. Fold. Garnish with whipped cream and shaved chocolate.

LIME PIE   Yield: Serves 4 to 6

1 (3-ounce) package lime gelatin
¾ cup boiling water
Juice of 2 limes
Grated rind of 2 limes
2 eggs, separated
1⅓ cups (15-ounce can) sweetened
   condensed milk

¼ teaspoon aromatic bitters
Few drops green food coloring
1 unbaked 10" chocolate crumb crust,
   chilled (see page 105)
Whipped topping (optional)
Shaved chocolate (optional)

Dissolve gelatin in boiling water. Add lime juice and rind to gelatin. Place steel cutting blade into container. Process egg yolks for 10 seconds. Slowly pour gelatin mixture, condensed milk, bitters, and food coloring through feed tube. Process until well blended. Pour into a large bowl and refrigerate until slightly thickened, about 20 to 30 minutes. In a small mixing bowl, beat egg whites with an electric mixer until light and fluffy. Fold egg whites into chilled gelatin mixture. Pour into prepared crust. Chill until firm. Garnish with whipped topping and shaved chocolate, if desired.

QUICK BLUEBERRY TORTE Yield: Serves 12 to 16

This is a dessert that looks as if it took much more time to prepare than it does.

2 eggs
1 (8-ounce) package cream cheese,
  cut into chunks
⅓ cup granulated sugar

1 unbaked graham cracker crust prepared
  in a 9″ x 9″ x 2″ pan (see page 105)
1 (21-ounce) can blueberry pie filling
Whipped cream (optional)

Preheat oven to 350°F. Place steel cutting blade into container. Add eggs and process until foamy. Add cream cheese and sugar. Process until thoroughly blended and smooth. Pour into prepared graham cracker crust. Bake for 25 minutes, or until top is set. Cool 10 minutes. Spread blueberry filling over cream cheese. Chill until serving time. Cut into 2¼″ squares. Garnish with whipped cream, if desired, and serve.

CHOCOLATE ÉCLAIRS Yield: Serves 12

CREAM PUFF PASTE

1 cup water
½ cup butter or margarine
¼ teaspoon salt

1 cup sifted all-purpose flour
4 eggs

Preheat oven to 400°F. In a saucepan, combine water, butter, and salt. Bring to a rolling boil. Add flour all at once. Stir vigorously, until a thick, smooth ball is formed which leaves the side of the pan clean. Remove from heat. Place steel cutting blade into container. Add mixture from saucepan. Add eggs, one at a time, processing between each addition, until well blended and smooth. On a large ungreased cookie sheet, shape into 12 (1″ x 4″) strips using either a pastry bag or a teaspoon. Bake for 40 minutes, or until puffed and golden brown. Remove from cookie sheet and cool completely on a wire rack.

FILLING

2 (3-ounce) packages instant vanilla
  pudding, divided

4 cups milk, divided

Place steel cutting blade into container. Add one package of pudding and 2 cups milk. Process until thickened. Pour into a bowl and repeat for the other package. Fill éclairs by slitting éclairs open and spooning filling in. You may wish to make a hole in the end of the éclair and fill, using a pastry bag.

GLAZE

2 squares unsweetened chocolate
3 tablespoons butter or margarine

2 cups sifted confectioners sugar
¼ cup boiling water

In a small saucepan over low heat, melt chocolate and butter. In a bowl, combine chocolate mixture with sugar and boiling water. Beat with wire whisk until smooth. Dip top of éclairs into glaze. Let set; refrigerate until serving.

CREAM CHEESE FROSTING   Yield: About ¾ cup

1 (3-ounce) package cream cheese,
 softened and cut into chunks
1 tablespoon butter or margarine, softened

2 teaspoons lemon juice
1 cup sifted confectioners sugar

Place steel cutting blade into container. Process cream cheese until smooth. Add butter and lemon juice. Process until thoroughly combined. Add confectioners sugar. Process until smooth, about 15 seconds. Use as a frosting on one-layer cakes.

MOCHA FROSTING   Yield: 1¼ cups

1 (1-ounce) square unsweetened chocolate
½ teaspoon instant coffee
1 tablespoon hot water (160° to 180°F)

3 tablespoons butter or margarine, softened
1 cup confectioners sugar
½ teaspoon vanilla extract

Melt chocolate in a double boiler. Set aside to cool. Dissolve instant coffee in hot water. Set aside to cool. Place steel cutting blade into container. Add butter. Process until smooth. Add confectioners sugar, vanilla extract, cooled chocolate, and coffee. Process until smooth and creamy. Use as a frosting on cookies or one-layer cakes.

CONFECTIONERS GLAZE   Yield: ⅔ cup

1½ cups sifted confectioners sugar
2 tablespoons butter or margarine,
 softened

½ teaspoon vanilla extract
2 to 3 tablespoons hot milk

Place steel cutting blade into container. Add confectioners sugar, butter, and vanilla extract. With processor running, pour 2 tablespoons hot milk down feed tube. Process until smooth. If a thinner glaze is desired, add an additional tablespoon hot milk and process. Drizzle over coffee cake or cookies.

FRESH LEMON FROSTING   Yield: About ¾ cup

2 cups confectioners sugar
1 teaspoon lemon rind

¼ cup lemon juice

Place steel cutting blade into container. Add confectioners sugar and lemon rind. While processor is running, pour lemon juice down feed tube. Use as a frosting on cookies or one-layer cakes.

GLOSSY CHOCOLATE FROSTING   Yield: About 1 cup

2 tablespoons butter or margarine,
  softened
1½ cups confectioners sugar
2 (1-ounce) squares unsweetened
  chocolate, melted

3 tablespoons water
2 teaspoons light corn syrup
1 teaspoon vanilla extract

Place steel cutting blade into container. Process butter and confectioners sugar until creamy. Add melted chocolate, water, corn syrup, and vanilla extract. Process until smooth. Use as a frosting on cookies, brownies, or one-layer cake.

CREAMY CHOCOLATE FROSTING   Yield: About ½ cup

3 tablespoons cocoa
⅓ cup confectioners sugar
2 tablespoons butter or margarine

2 tablespoons cream cheese
½ teaspoon vanilla extract

Place steel cutting blade into container. Process all ingredients until smooth. Use as a frosting for cookies, brownies, or one-layer cakes.

THE VEGETABLE STAND

Chapter Six

Have vegetables fresh, cold, and crisp to start processing and then let your imagination soar. The processor will amaze you with its speed and efficiency in slicing eggplant, zucchini, and other vegetables — zip! and they are ready for Ratatouille, Tater 'n' Onions, or Layered Zucchini Casserole. You just put the dishes together, cook, and enjoy them.

SKILLET EGGPLANT   Yield: Serves 4 to 6

2 slices oven-dried white bread,
  quartered
½ teaspoon salt
⅛ teaspoon pepper

1 medium eggplant, peeled
  and cut into wedges
1 slightly beaten egg
1 tablespoon milk

Place steel cutting blade into container. Add bread, salt, and pepper. Process until finely crumbed. Empty into small bowl. Place slicing disc into container. Slice eggplant. Empty onto a sheet of waxed paper. In a small dish, combine egg and milk. Dip eggplant slices into egg mixture, then into bread crumb mixture. Fry eggplant in hot oil in large skillet for 3 minutes on each side, or until browned and tender. Drain on paper towels. Keep eggplant warm in 300°F oven while frying remaining eggplant. Serve warm.

RATATOUILLE   Yield: Serves 4 to 5

A casserole combining eggplant, zucchini, tomato, and green pepper with seasonings and topped with Parmesan cheese.

1 green pepper, cored
1 medium onion, peeled
1 clove garlic, peeled and crushed
2 tablespoons olive oil
2 small zucchini, trimmed
½ medium eggplant, peeled
  and cut into wedges
1 cup tomato wedges, peeled and seeded

¾ teaspoon salt
½ teaspoon basil
¼ teaspoon oregano
Dash of black pepper
1 tablespoon cornstarch
1 tablespoon water
1 ounce Parmesan cheese, cut into 1" cubes
Parsley (optional)

Place slicing disc into container. Slice green pepper and onion. Add garlic. Sauté in saucepan, in olive oil, until tender. Place slicing disc into container. Slice zucchini and eggplant. Add to sautéed pepper and onion mixture. Add tomatoes, salt, basil, oregano, and pepper. Cover and cook over low heat 20 to 30 minutes, until tender, stirring occasionally. Remove from heat. Combine cornstarch and water; gradually stir into vegetables. Cook until thickened. Transfer to a 1½-quart casserole. Place steel cutting blade into container. Process Parmesan cheese until finely grated. Sprinkle cheese over vegetables. Broil until cheese is lightly browned. Garnish with parsley, if desired, and serve immediately.

ORANGE-GLAZED SWEET POTATOES   Yield: Serves 3 to 4

A good-tasting sweet potato dish. Serve with ham, chicken or turkey.

5 small sweet potatoes, peeled   ½ cup brown sugar, firmly packed
3 tablespoons butter or margarine   2 tablespoons orange juice

Place slicing disc into container. Slice potatoes. Place in saucepan of boiling salt water. Cook until tender, approximately 15 minutes. In a saucepan, melt butter. Add brown sugar, and orange juice. Stir until sugar is dissolved. Boil for 1 minute. Drain potatoes and add to glaze. Toss gently until well coated. Serve immediately.

SAUTÉED MUSHROOMS   Yield: Serves 4

¼ cup butter or margarine   Salt and pepper to taste
1 pound fresh mushrooms

In a large frypan, over low heat, melt butter. Place slicing disc into container. Slice mushrooms. Add sliced mushrooms to frypan. Sauté, stirring frequently, for about 5 to 10 minutes. Serve hot.

Serving Suggestion: Serve with steak.

MINI-SHOESTRING POTATOES   Yield: About 2 cups

The shredding disc saves your hands and shreds potatoes perfectly.

2 medium potatoes, peeled   Salt to taste
Oil for frying

Place shredding disc into container. Shred potatoes. Add potatoes to a bowl of cold water and allow to stand for 1 hour. Heat oil in deep fryer to desired temperature. Drain potatoes and pat dry with paper towels. Fry in heated oil. Serve as a snack or as a casserole topping.

AU GRATIN POTATOES Yield: Serves 4 to 6

A pleasing potato dish to serve with halibut steak.

4 medium potatoes, peeled
8 ounces American cheese
¼ cup butter or margarine
¼ cup sifted all-purpose flour

2 cups milk
¼ teaspoon salt
Dash of pepper

Preheat oven to 350°F. Place slicing disc into container. Slice whole potatoes. Place potato slices in saucepan and cover with water. Cook until potatoes are tender. Drain off water. Set potatoes aside. Place shredding disc into container. Shred cheese. Empty cheese onto waxed paper. In a saucepan, over low heat, melt butter and stir in flour. Slowly add milk, stirring until smooth. Continue stirring until mixture thickens. Add salt and pepper, and shredded cheese. Stir until cheese melts. Place cooked potatoes in a 2½-quart casserole. Pour cheese mixture over potatoes. Bake for 30 to 35 minutes, until potatoes are tender and cheese is golden brown. Serve hot.

BROCCOLI CASSEROLE Yield: Serves 5 to 6

Broccoli prepared in a distinctive manner — an excellent side dish with seafood.

1 (20-ounce) package frozen broccoli
8 ounces charp Cheddar cheese
4 slices bread, quartered

3 tablespoons butter or margarine
1 tablespoon grated lemon peel
Salt and pepper to taste

Preheat oven to 350°F. Cook broccoli according to package directions. Drain and set aside. Place shredding disc into container. Shred cheese. Empty onto a sheet of waxed paper. Place steel cutting blade into container. Add bread and process until crumbs are formed. In a large frypan, melt butter over medium heat. Add bread crumbs and lemon peel. Continue cooking until bread crumbs have browned. In a 2½-quart casserole, layer broccoli and shredded cheese. Top with bread crumbs. Bake for 25 to 30 minutes. Serve hot.

BUTTERNUT SQUASH AND APPLE BAKE   Yield: Serves 5 to 6

This winter squash casserole is a good choice to serve with roast turkey and chicken.

1 (1½- to 2-pound) butternut squash,
   peeled, cut into wedges, and seeded
2 medium cooking apples, cored
   and quartered
½ cup brown sugar, firmly packed

¼ cup butter or margarine, melted
1 tablespoon sifted all-purpose flour
1 teaspoon cinnamon
½ teaspoon salt

Preheat oven to 350°F. Place slicing disc into container. Slice squash and apples. Pour into an ungreased 8" x 8" x 2" baking pan. Stir until well mixed. Place steel cutting blade into container. Add brown sugar, flour, cinnamon, and salt. Process adding butter through feed tube, until blended. Sprinkle brown sugar mixture over squash and apples. Cover with aluminum foil. Bake 50 minutes, or until squash is tender. Serve hot.

Variation: Add ½ cup chopped nuts.

POTATO PANCAKES   Yield: Serves 2 to 3

Serve these pancakes with braised meats, or as a lunch dish with applesauce.

Oil for frying
3 medium potatoes, peeled
1 medium onion, peeled and quartered
1 egg

1 tablespoon + 1 teaspoon sifted
   all-purpose flour
¼ teaspoon baking powder
¼ teaspoon salt
Dash of pepper

Preheat oil in frypan. Place shredding disc into container. Shred potatoes. Empty into a colander; drain well. Place steel cutting blade into container. Add onion. Process until finely chopped. Add egg, flour, baking powder, salt, and pepper. Process until well blended. Add shredded potatoes. Process, using TOUCH-ON control, until potatoes are coarsely chopped. Drop by heaping table-spoonfuls into hot frypan. Fry on each side until golden brown. Serve hot.

Serving Suggestion: Serve with applesauce or sour cream.

SAUTÉED ONIONS   Yield: Serves 2 to 3

4 small onions, peeled   3 tablespoons butter or margarine

Place slicing disc into container. Slice onions. In a frypan, over low heat, melt butter. Add onions and sauté, stirring frequently until golden brown. Serve immediately with hamburgers, steak, or liver.

COTTAGE FRIES   Yield: Serves 4 to 6

This is an appetizing way to prepare potatoes.

4 medium potatoes, peeled   ½ teaspoon salt
2 tablespoons butter or margarine   Dash of pepper
1 tablespoon shortening

Place slicing disc into container. Slice potatoes. Melt butter and shortening over low heat in frypan. Add potato slices and season with salt and pepper. Cook until a brown crust forms on potatoes. Turn and cook until brown crust forms on other side. Serve hot.

TATERS 'N' ONIONS   Yield: Serves 6 to 8

Hash browns with a little more tang.

6 large potatoes, peeled and quartered   3 tablespoons shortening
1 small onion, peeled   1 teaspoon salt
1 clove garlic, peeled and halved   ¼ teaspoon pepper

Place slicing disc into container. Slice potatoes and onion. Rub a frypan with garlic. Place frypan over low heat. Add shortening. When shortening has melted, add potatoes, onions, salt, and pepper. Cook, stirring occasionally, until potatoes are evenly browned and tender, about 25 to 30 minutes. Serve hot.

GOLDEN CARROTS   Yield: Serves 3 to 4

Chopped carrots, delicately flavored, to serve with meat.

¼ cup parsley sprigs
6 to 8 medium carrots, peeled
3 tablespoons butter or margarine

¼ teaspoon salt
¼ teaspoon ginger

Place steel cutting blade into container. Add parsley. Process until chopped. Empty onto waxed paper. Place steel cutting blade into container. Add carrots. Process until finely chopped. Melt butter in a saucepan. Add chopped carrots, salt, and ginger. Cover and cook over medium heat for 20 minutes or until tender. Garnish with chopped parsley.

BAKED GERMAN POTATO SALAD   Yield: Serves 8 to 10

This is a hot potato salad, excellent with ham, sausage, corned beef, or tongue.

6 slices bacon
1 small onion, peeled and quartered
2 tablespoons sifted all-purpose flour
1 tablespoon granulated sugar
1 teaspoon salt

¼ teaspoon black pepper
½ teaspoon celery seed
⅓ cup cider vinegar
¾ cup water
6 medium potatoes, peeled

Preheat oven to 400°F. In a large frypan, fry bacon until crisp; reserve drippings. Drain bacon on paper towels. Place steel cutting blade into container. Coarsely crumble bacon, using the TOUCH-ON control. Empty onto waxed paper. Place onion in container; process until coarsely chopped. Sauté onion in reserved bacon drippings until tender. Blend in flour, sugar, salt, pepper, celery seed, then add vinegar and water. Stir until thickened. Reduce heat. Place slicing disc in container. Slice potatoes. Transfer sliced potatoes to skillet; add crumbled bacon. Toss lightly to coat potatoes. Bake mixture in a covered 2-quart casserole for 60 to 75 minutes, or until potatoes are tender. Serve hot.

FRENCH-FRIED ONION RINGS   Yield: Serves 4 to 6

A "must" with steak, these onions are fried until they are crisp and golden.

4 small onions, peeled
2 eggs
⅔ cup milk
2 tablespoons butter or margarine,
    softened

1 cup sifted all-purpose flour
1 teaspoon baking powder
½ teaspoon salt
Oil for frying

Heat oil to desired temperature in deep fryer. Place slicing disc into container. Slice onions. Empty onto waxed paper. Separate into rings. Place steel cutting blade into container. Add eggs, milk, and butter. Process for 20 seconds. Remove cover and sift flour, baking powder, and salt into container. Process until mixture is smooth. Dip onion rings into batter. Allow excess batter to drain. Fry, a few at a time, in heated oil, until golden brown. Serve hot.

FRENCH-FRIED POTATOES   Yield: Serves 4 to 6

Your French-fry cutter prepares these potatoes for deep frying.

4 medium potatoes, peeled and halved
Salt to taste

Oil for frying

Heat oil to desired temperature in deep fryer. Place French-fry cutter into container. Pack potatoes sideways in feed tube and process. Remove excess moisture from potatoes by patting with paper towels. Fry a few at a time, in heated oil, until golden brown. Drain on paper towels. Sprinkle with salt. Serve hot.

LAYERED ZUCCHINI CASSEROLE Yield: Serves 4 to 6

Make full use of your food processor in preparing the ingredients for this casserole.

8 ounces Cheddar cheese
2 to 3 small zucchini
3 medium, firm tomatoes
1 small onion, peeled

3 slices bread, quartered
2 tablespoons butter or margarine, melted
2 tablespoons grated Parmesan cheese
Salt and pepper to taste

Preheat oven to 350°F. Grease a 1½-quart casserole dish. Place shredding disc into container. Shred Cheddar cheese. Empty onto a sheet of waxed paper. Place slicing disc into container. Slice zucchini, tomatoes, and onion. Empty onto a separate sheet of waxed paper. Place steel cutting blade into container. Add bread and process until finely crumbed. Add butter and Parmesan cheese. Process until combined. In casserole dish, layer half of the zucchini slices, followed by half the tomato slices and half the onion slices. Sprinkle with salt and pepper, and 1 cup of shredded Cheddar cheese. Layer remaining zucchini, tomato, and onion. Sprinkle with salt, pepper, and remaining Cheddar cheese. Sprinkle bread crumb mixture over the cheese. Bake for 30 to 40 minutes or until vegetables are tender.

THE DAIRY BAR

Chapter Seven

Use your food processor to mix up some flavored butters to have on hand. Keep them ready for use as spreads, toppings for vegetables, or as condiments with meat or fish. Swiftly shred cheese for Welsh Rabbit, Cheese Strata, or Cheese Soufflé. Cheese and egg dishes, combined or apart, are welcome to the palate from morning to night, and the food processor makes them more easily managed than ever.

FRESH AND CREAMY BUTTER   Yield: About ½ cup

1 cup whipping cream, well chilled   ¼ to ½ teaspoon salt (optional)

Place steel cutting blade into container. Add whipping cream. Process until butter is formed, approximately 2½ minutes. Empty into colander and press out remaining liquid. Place in a container. Blend in salt, if desired. Cover and refrigerate up to 1 week.

ZESTY BUTTER   Yield: About ½ cup

½ cup butter, softened   1½ to 2 teaspoons Italian dressing mix

Place steel cutting blade into container. Add butter. Process until smooth. Add Italian dressing mix. Process until well blended.

Serving Suggestion: Spread on French bread and place under broiler until bubbly.

MUSTARD BUTTER   Yield: ½ cup

½ cup butter or margarine, softened   1 tablespoon mustard

Place steel cutting blade into container. Add butter and mustard. Process until smooth. Use as a spread on sandwiches.

DILL BUTTER   Yield: ½ cup

½ cup butter or margarine, softened   2 teaspoons dill weed

Place steel cutting blade into container. Add butter and dill weed. Process until smooth. Use as a topping on vegetables or as a condiment with meat.

ORANGE BUTTER   Yield: ½ cup

½ cup butter or margarine, softened   ½ teaspoon grated orange rind
1 teaspoon freshly squeezed   1 tablespoon confectioners sugar
    orange juice

Place steel cutting blade into container. Add butter, orange juice, orange rind, and confectioners sugar. Process until smooth. Use as a spread on waffles, pancakes, or toast.

GARLIC BUTTER   Yield: ½ cup

½ cup butter or margarine, softened   1 clove garlic

Place steel cutting blade into container. Add butter and garlic. Process until smooth. Use as a spread on Italian bread.

PEANUT BUTTER   Yield: ¾ cup

8 ounces salted cocktail-style peanuts

Place steel cutting blade into container. Add peanuts. Process until smooth. Serve on crackers or on bread for sandwiches.

Variation: Add 1 tablespoon honey or vegetable oil to peanuts while processing to improve spreading.

CASHEW BUTTER   Yield: ¾ cup

8 ounces roasted, salted cashews

Place steel cutting blade into container. Add cashews. Process until smooth. Serve on assorted crackers.

MAPLE BUTTER   Yield: ½ cup

½ cup butter or margarine, softened   3 tablespoons maple-flavored syrup

Place steel cutting blade into container. Process butter and syrup until smooth. Serve on waffles or pancakes.

CHEDDAR BUTTER   Yield: About 1¼ cups

3 to 4 ounces Cheddar cheese   ¼ teaspoon onion powder (optional)
½ cup butter or margarine, chilled,
   cut into 1" pieces

Place shredding disc into container. Shred cheese. Empty onto sheet of waxed paper. Place steel cutting blade into container. Add butter, shredded cheese, and onion powder, if desired. Process until smooth and creamy. Serve at room temperature on breads or vegetables.

RAISIN AND CHIP CHEESE SPREAD   Yield: About 1 cup

8 ounces cream cheese, cut into chunks
2 teaspoons milk
¾ teaspoon vanilla extract
1 tablespoon + 1 teaspoon
   confectioners sugar

1 to 2 tablespoons semi-sweet
   chocolate morsels
1 to 2 tablespoons seedless raisins

Place steel cutting blade into container. Add cream cheese, milk, vanilla extract, and sugar. Process until creamy. Add chocolate morsels and raisins. Process until well blended. Serve chilled with crackers.

CINNAMON FRENCH TOAST   Yield: Serves 4

4 eggs
½ teaspoon salt
2 tablespoons granulated sugar
½ cup milk

½ teaspoon cinnamon
8 slices bread
2 tablespoons butter or margarine

Place steel cutting blade into container. Add eggs, salt, sugar, milk, and cinnamon. Process until well blended. Pour into a shallow bowl. Heat butter in a frypan until melted. Dip bread into egg mixture. Add bread to heated frypan. Cook bread on each side until golden brown. Serve hot.

APPLE-CINNAMON PANCAKES   Yield: Serves 6 to 8

The food processor shines when it comes to chopping apples and nuts.

Oil for cooking
1 large, tart, cooking apple,
   peeled and quartered
¼ cup nuts
1 egg
1¾ cups milk

2 cups sifted all-purpose flour
2 teaspoons baking powder
1 teaspoon salt
2 tablespoons granulated sugar
1 teaspoon cinnamon
3 tablespoons butter, melted

Preheat lightly oiled griddle to desired temperature. Place steel cutting blade into container. Coarsely chop apple. Empty onto waxed paper. Coarsely chop nuts. Empty onto waxed paper. Place steel cutting blade into container. Add egg and milk. Process until foamy. Remove cover and sift flour, baking powder, salt, sugar, and cinnamon into container. Process only until combined. Add melted butter. Process until blended. Add apple mixture. Process, using TOUCH-ON control, until just blended. DO NOT OVERPROCESS. Pour about 3 tablespoons batter onto heated griddle. Cook pancakes on each side until golden brown. Serve hot.

EGG AND POTATO BAKE   Yield: Serves 4 to 6

This main dish casserole is very good.

1 medium potato, peeled and halved
1 small onion, peeled
2 tablespoons butter or margarine
4 ounces Cheddar cheese

1 cup ham, cut into 1" cubes
6 parsley sprigs
4 eggs

Preheat oven to 350°F. Grease a 9" x 9" x 2" baking pan. Place slicing disc into container. Slice potato and onion. Melt butter over medium heat in a frypan and add potato and onion slices. Cook until tender. Spoon cooked potato mixture into prepared baking pan. Place shredding disc into container. Shred cheese. Empty onto waxed paper. Place steel cutting blade into container. Add ham and parsley. Process until coarsely chopped. Spoon onto potato mixture. Place steel cutting blade into container and add eggs. Process until light in color. Pour over potato mixture. Sprinkle with shredded cheese. Bake for 20 to 25 minutes, or until set. Serve hot.

VEGETARIAN SCRAMBLED EGGS   Yield: Serves 4

Sunday night scrambled eggs made glorious with cheese, mushrooms, scallions, and tomato.

8 ounces Swiss cheese
½ pound mushrooms
2 scallions
5 tablespoons butter, divided

8 eggs
½ cup milk
½ teaspoon salt
1 tomato, diced

Place shredding disc into container. Shred cheese. Empty onto a sheet of waxed paper. Place slicing disc into container. Slice mushrooms and scallions. Melt 2 tablespoons butter in frypan. Sauté mushrooms and scallions until tender. Place steel cutting blade into container. Add eggs, milk, and salt. Process until well blended. In another frypan, melt remaining butter. Add egg mixture. Scramble eggs over medium heat until they begin to set. Add shredded cheese, mushroom mixture, and tomato. Reduce heat and stir until cheese is melted. Serve immediately.

PROCESSOR GRIDDLE CAKES   Yield: Serves 5 to 6

1 egg
1½ cups milk
2 cups sifted all-purpose flour
1 tablespoon baking powder

2 tablespoons granulated sugar
1 teaspoon salt
3 tablespoons butter or margarine, melted

Place steel cutting blade into container. Add egg and milk. Process until foamy. Sift flour, baking powder, sugar, and salt into container. Process only until blended, about 3 seconds. Pour melted butter through feed tube. Process only until blended. Drop batter by spoonfuls onto heated griddle. Brown on each side. Serve immediately.

Variations:

Pecan Griddle Cakes: Add ¾ cup finely chopped pecans to batter and blend in.

Banana Griddle Cakes: Before turning griddle cakes, put 3 or 4 thin slices of banana on each cake. Turn and finish browning. Serve with butter, sugar, and cinnamon, or sugar mixed with grated lemon peel.

Pineapple Griddle Cakes: Before turning griddle cakes, put 1 spoonful of crushed pineapple on each cake. Turn and finish browning.

Strawberry Griddle Cakes: Before turning griddle cakes, put 4 thin slices fresh strawberries on each cake. Turn and finish browning. Serve with strawberry syrup.

ORANGE-PECAN WAFFLES   Yield: Serves 6 to 8

½ cup shelled pecans
2 large eggs
¾ cup milk
¼ cup orange juice
1 tablespoon grated orange rind
½ teaspoon vanilla extract

1½ cups sifted all-purpose flour
2½ teaspoons baking powder
1 tablespoon granulated sugar
½ teaspoon salt
⅓ cup melted butter or margarine, cooled

Preheat waffle iron to desired temperature. Place steel cutting blade into container. Coarsely chop the pecans. Empty onto a sheet of waxed paper. Add eggs. Process until foamy. Add milk, orange juice, orange rind, and vanilla extract. Process until combined. Sift flour, baking powder, sugar, and salt into container. Process until thoroughly blended. Remove cover and scrape down container sides. Add butter and pecans to batter. Process until only blended. DO NOT OVERPROCESS. Bake in preheated waffle iron until golden brown.

SWEDISH PANCAKES   Yield: Serves 3 to 4

6 eggs
⅓ cup milk
1 teaspoon vanilla extract
⅓ cup sifted all-purpose flour

¼ cup granulated sugar
2 tablespoons butter, melted
Jam
Sour cream

Place steel cutting blade into container. Add eggs, milk, and vanilla extract. Process until foamy. Add flour and sugar. Process until blended. Pour melted butter through feed tube. Process only until blended. Pour a scant ¼ cup of batter into preheated, lightly oiled, 8″ sloped-edge frypan and tilt to coat interior of pan. Fry pancake until edges turn light brown. Gently lift and turn pancake with spatula. Fry second side until lightly browned, about ½ minute. Second side will have mottled appearance. Fill pancake with jam. Roll in spiral motion and top with sour cream.

CHEESE SOUFFLÉ   Yield: Serves 5 to 6

Soufflés must be served immediately after they are done or they fall, so plan accordingly.

6 ounces sharp Cheddar cheese, chilled
2 ounces Parmesan cheese, cut in 1″ cubes
⅓ cup butter or margarine
1 small onion, peeled and quartered
⅓ cup sifted all-purpose flour

1 teaspoon dry mustard
1½ cups milk
6 eggs, separated
¼ teaspoon cream of tartar

Preheat oven to 350°F. Place shredding disc into container. Shred Cheddar cheese. Empty onto a sheet of waxed paper. Butter a 2½-quart soufflé dish or casserole. Place steel cutting blade into container. Add Parmesan cheese. Process until cheese is finely grated. Sprinkle 2 tablespoons Parmesan over bottom and sides of buttered dish. Set aside. Empty remaining Parmesan onto a sheet of waxed paper. In a saucepan, melt butter. Place steel cutting blade into container. Add onion. Process until finely chopped. Add to saucepan. Sauté the onion until lightly browned. Stir in flour and dry mustard. Cook until bubbly. Add milk. Cook over medium-high heat until mixture comes to a boil, stirring constantly. Remove saucepan from heat. Add cheeses. Stir until melted. Place steel cutting blade into container. Add egg yolks. Process until thick and lemon colored. Stir a small amount of hot cheese mixture into egg yolks. Pour into saucepan. Stir until well blended. Using a mixer, beat the egg whites and cream of tartar until stiff (but not dry). Fold beaten egg whites into cheese mixture. Pour into prepared dish. Holding a spoon upright, make a ring 1″ deep and 1″ from sides of dish. Bake for 35 to 40 minutes, or until puffy and delicately browned. Soufflé should shake very slightly when oven rack is moved back and forth. Serve immediately.

WELSH RABBIT   Yield: Serves 3 to 4

A favorite dish from the English. Keep it hot in a chafing dish for an after-the-theater or game party.

12 ounces Cheddar cheese	⅛ teaspoon salt
3 tablespoons butter or margarine	1 cup milk
3 tablespoons sifted all-purpose flour	¼ cup wine
¼ teaspoon dry mustard	

Place shredding disc into container. Shred cheese. Empty cheese onto a sheet of waxed paper. Melt butter in saucepan. Stir in flour, dry mustard, and salt. Cook over low heat until mixture bubbles. Slowly add milk, stirring constantly until mixture is very thick. Gradually add wine; stir in cheese. Continue stirring until cheese melts. Serve warm over toast.

Serving Suggestion: Serve over tomato slices and cooked bacon on toast.

CHEESE STRATA   Yield: Serves 4

An impressive looking cheese casserole that's unbelievably simple to make. A delicious choice for brunch.

8 slices white bread, crusts removed	1¾ cups milk
Butter or margarine, softened	¾ teaspoon salt
10 ounces mild Cheddar cheese	Dash of pepper
3 eggs	½ teaspoon dry mustard

Spread both sides of bread with butter. Place 4 slices in 1 layer in a greased 9″ x 9″ x 2″ pan. Place shredding disc into container. Shred cheese. Sprinkle half of cheese evenly over bread. Cover with 4 remaining bread slices and sprinkle with remaining cheese. Place steel cutting blade into container. Add eggs, milk, salt, pepper, and dry mustard. Process until well blended. Pour over cheese and bread. Refrigerate for 4 hours. Preheat oven to 325°F. Bake for 60 to 75 minutes or until puffed and browned.

OMELET   Yield: Serves 4 to 6

6 eggs	⅛ teaspoon pepper
6 tablespoons cold water	2 tablespoons butter or margarine
½ teaspoon salt	

Place steel cutting blade into container. Add eggs, cold water, salt, and pepper. Process until well blended. In a large frypan over low heat, melt butter. Tilt frypan to grease bottom and sides. Pour eggs into frypan. As omelet sets, lift edges with spatula and tilt pan so uncooked mixture spreads underneath. Repeat until omelet is cooked. Spread with desired filling. Loosen omelet edge all around with spatula. Fold one side of omelet over other side of omelet to hold in filling. Roll out onto heated platter. Serve immediately.

FILLINGS

Onion-Bacon-Swiss Cheese filling: Place steel cutting blade into container. Add ¼ medium onion and 4 slices cooked bacon. Process until coarsely chopped. Empty onto a sheet of waxed paper. Place shredding disc into container. Shred 3 ounces Swiss cheese. Add onion, bacon, and Swiss cheese to cooked omelet before folding over.

Ham-Green Pepper-Mushrooms filling: Place steel cutting blade into container. Add ¼ green pepper, and ½ cup ham, cut into cubes. Process until coarsely chopped. Empty container onto a sheet of waxed paper. Place slicing disc into container. Add 3 ounces mushrooms. Slice mushrooms. Add ham, green pepper, and mushrooms to cooked omelet before folding over.

Green Pepper-Onion-Muenster Cheese filling: Place steel cutting blade into container. Add ¼ green pepper, and ¼ medium onion. Process until coarsely chopped. Empty onto a sheet of waxed paper. Place shredding disc into container. Shred 3 ounces Muenster cheese. Add green pepper, onion, and Muenster cheese to cooked omelet before folding over.

THE
SWEET
SHOP

Chapter Eight

Satisfy your sweet tooth with the recipes in this chapter. The food processor is in its element chopping nuts for Nutty Fudge Squares. It will help you with any of the inviting recipes — to make them chewy or smooth, refreshing, and delectable as manna.

DESSERT CRÊPES Yield: 12 to 14 crêpes

Thin French pancakes to be filled with dessert-type foods.

4 eggs
½ cup milk
½ cup water
1 teaspoon vanilla

2 tablespoons butter or margarine, melted
½ teaspoon salt
2 teaspoons granulated sugar
1 cup sifted all-purpose flour

Place steel cutting blade into container. Add all ingredients. Process about 5 seconds, until just combined. Follow crêpemaker cooking directions or: Preheat an 8″ sloped-edge pan. Grease pan lightly. Pour a scant ¼ cup of batter into pan to coat interior. Fry until edges turn light brown and batter no longer steams. Using a fork or spatula, gently loosen edges. Remove from pan. Stack on plate.

CHEESY CRÊPES Yield: Serves 8 to 10

This French pancake holds a savory two-cheese mixture.

1 cup Ricotta cheese
⅔ cup cottage cheese
¼ cup confectioners sugar
½ teaspoon vanilla extract

½ teaspoon grated lemon peel
8 to 10 prepared dessert crêpes, (see above)
Additional confectioners sugar
Strawberry preserves

Preheat oven to 300°F. Grease an 8″ x 8″ x 2″ baking pan. Place steel cutting blade into container. Add Ricotta cheese, cottage cheese, confectioners sugar, vanilla extract, and lemon peel. Process until well blended. Spoon onto crêpes. Fold and place into prepared pan. Bake for 5 to 10 minutes, until warm. Sprinkle with confectioners sugar. Top with strawberry preserves. Serve immediately.

CANNOLI Yield: Serves 8

A dessert crêpe with a Ricotta cheese filling.

2 ounces pistachio nuts, shelled
1 (15-ounce) container Ricotta cheese
⅓ cup granulated sugar
1 teaspoon ground cinnamon

1 teaspoon vanilla extract
½ cup confectioners sugar
8 dessert crêpes (see above)

Place steel cutting blade into container. Coarsely chop pistachio nuts. Empty onto a sheet of waxed paper. Place steel cutting blade into container. Add Ricotta cheese, sugar, cinnamon, and vanilla extract. Process until smooth. Fill dessert crêpes with 2 tablespoons of mixture. Freeze until ready to serve. When serving, sprinkle crêpe with chopped nuts and confectioners sugar.

CREAMY LEMON CRÊPES   Yield: Serves 3 to 4

Lemon-flavored cream cheese fills these crêpes.

2 (3-ounce) packages cream cheese, cut
   into chunks
2 tablespoons milk
5 tablespoons confectioners sugar, divided

1 tablespoon lemon rind
1 teaspoon lemon juice
6 to 8 prepared dessert crêpes (see page 133)

Place steel cutting blade into container. Process cream cheese until softened. Add milk and 3 tablespoons confectioners sugar. Process until blended, scraping down container sides as necessary. Add lemon rind and lemon juice. Process until smooth. Thinly spread dessert crêpes with cream cheese mixture. Roll into a spiral roll then dust with remaining confectioners sugar. Serve immediately.

APPLE-RAISIN CRÊPES   Yield: Serves 3 to 4

A sauce to serve over dessert crêpes.

2 large, tart, cooking apples,
   peeled, cored, and quartered
3 tablespoons butter or margarine
¼ cup brown sugar, firmly packed

½ cup raisins
½ teaspoon cinnamon
Dash of nutmeg
6 to 8 dessert crêpes (see page 133)

Place slicing disc into container. Slice apples. Melt butter in a frypan, over low heat and add apples. Stir until apples are coated with melted butter. Add brown sugar, raisins, cinnamon, and nutmeg. Heat thoroughly. Spoon onto crêpes. Fold and serve immediately.

Serving Suggestion: Garnish with whipped topping or whipped cream and sprinkle with cinnamon.

FRESH FRUIT CRÊPES   Yield: Serves 4 to 6

2 firm bananas
1 pint fresh strawberries, hulled

1 tablespoon lemon juice
4 to 6 prepared dessert crêpes (see page 133)

Place slicing disc into container. Slice bananas and strawberries. Empty into small bowl. Add lemon juice to fruit; toss lightly. Spoon onto dessert crêpes. Fold and serve.

Suggested Topping: Fruit and Honey Dressing (see page 62).

CHOCOLATE CHIP ICE CREAM PIE   Yield: Serves 10 to 12

Chocolaty goodness from crust to topping.

CRUST

1½ cups sifted all-purpose flour
½ teaspoon salt
½ teaspoon baking soda
½ cup butter or margarine,
   cut into chunks

½ cup brown sugar, packed
⅓ cup granulated sugar
1 egg
½ teaspoon vanilla extract
1 (6-ounce) package chocolate chips

Preheat oven to 350°F. Grease a 13" x 9" x 2" baking pan. Place steel cutting blade into container. Sift flour, salt, and baking soda into container. Add butter, sugars, egg, and vanilla extract and process until well blended. Empty dough into a bowl and stir in chocolate chips. Refrigerate until dough is easy to handle. Press dough into bottom of prepared pan. Bake for 10 to 15 minutes, or until lightly browned. Cool in pan on wire rack.

TOPPING

½ gallon vanilla ice cream, divided   ¼ cup chocolate syrup

Place steel cutting blade into container. Divide ice cream into 2 parts. Add half of the ice cream and process until smooth. Spread onto crust. Repeat for remainder of ice cream. Drizzle with chocolate syrup. Freeze until firm.

PEACH SHAKE   Yield: Serves 1

2 canned peach halves, drained
2 large scoops vanilla ice cream

2 tablespoons syrup from fruit
¼ cup milk

Place steel cutting blade into container. Add peach halves. Process until puréed. Add ice cream, syrup, and milk. Process using TOUCH-ON control until smooth and creamy. Pour into a tall glass.

BANANA SHAKE   Yield: Serves 2

1 banana, cut into 1" chunks
1 pint vanilla ice cream, cut into chunks

3 tablespoons milk

Place steel cutting blade into container, add banana chunks. Process until puréed. Add ice cream and milk. Process, using TOUCH-ON control, until smooth and creamy. Pour into tall glasses.

CHOCOLATE-BANANA SHAKE   Yield: Serves 1 to 2

1 banana, cut into 1" chunks
4 scoops chocolate ice cream

3 tablespoons milk

Place steel cutting blade into container. Add banana chunks. Process until puréed. Add ice cream and milk. Process, using TOUCH-ON control, until smooth and creamy. Pour into tall glasses.

CHOCOLATE LOVER'S DELIGHT   Yield: Serves 2

½ pint vanilla ice cream,
  cut into chunks

2 to 4 tablespoons chocolate syrup
½ cup milk

Place steel cutting blade into container. Add ice cream, chocolate syrup, and milk. Process, using TOUCH-ON control, until smooth and creamy. Pour into tall glasses.

FUDGE-MINT MELTAWAYS   Yield: Serves 24

1 graham cracker 8″ crust recipe
 (see page 105)
1 (12-ounce) jar fudge or milk chocolate
 sauce

3 pints mint chocolate chip ice cream,
 cut into chunks
Shaved chocolate (optional)

Line 24 muffin cups with paper liners. Place 1 tablespoon of crust mixture in each liner and pat to line bottom. Place in freezer for ½ hour. Remove from freezer. Spread 1 heaping teaspoon of fudge sauce over each crust. Freeze for 1 hour. Before removing from freezer, place steel cutting blade into container. Add half of ice cream. Process just until smooth. Divide among 12 muffin cups. Repeat with remaining ice cream. Garnish with chocolate shavings, if desired. Freeze until firm.

COFFEE-FUDGE PIE   Yield: Serves 6 to 8

1 unbaked 9″ graham cracker crust
 (see page 105)
½ cup fudge or milk chocolate sauce

1 quart coffee ice cream, cut into chunks
Additional fudge sauce (optional)

Place prepared crust in freezer for ½ hour. Remove from freezer and spread fudge sauce over crust. Return to freezer for ½ hour. Just before removing crust from freezer, place steel cutting blade into container. Add ice cream. Process until smooth. Spread over fudge layer. Place in freezer until frozen. Drizzle with fudge sauce before serving, if desired.

BANANA SPLIT CUPS   Yield: Serves 24

1 graham cracker 8″ crust recipe
 (see page 105)
1 (12-ounce) jar fudge or milk chocolate
 sauce

1 firm banana, peeled and cut in half
3 pints vanilla ice cream, cut into chunks
¼ cup chopped walnuts
24 maraschino cherries

Line 24 muffin cups with paper liners. Place 1 tablespoon of crust mixture into each liner and pat to line bottom. Place in freezer for ½ hour. Remove from freezer. Spread 1 heaping teaspoon of fudge sauce over each crust. Freeze for 1 hour. Before removing from freezer, place slicing disc into container. Slice banana and empty onto a piece of waxed paper. Place steel cutting blade into container. Add half of the ice cream. Process, using TOUCH-ON control, until smooth. Divide banana slices among 24 muffin cups; divide ice cream among 12 muffin cups. Repeat with remaining ice cream. Drizzle fudge over top. Sprinkle with chopped nuts. Top with a cherry. Freeze until firm.

STRAWBERRY SHAKE   Yield: Serves 2

1 pint fresh strawberries,
  hulled
3 to 4 tablespoons granulated sugar

1 pint vanilla ice cream, cut in chunks
½ cup milk
2 whole strawberries (optional)

Combine strawberries and sugar in a bowl. Allow to rest for at least 15 minutes. Place steel cutting blade into container. Add strawberry mixture. Process, using TOUCH-ON control, until strawberries are slightly puréed. Add ice cream and milk. Process, using TOUCH-ON control, until smooth and creamy. Pour into tall glasses and garnish with whole strawberries, if desired.

SUNSHINE ORANGE FREEZE   Yield: Serves 2 to 3

1 (6-ounce) can frozen orange juice
  concentrate
2 cans water

1 pint vanilla ice cream, cut into chunks
1 orange, thickly sliced (optional)

In a separate container, prepare orange juice using orange juice concentrate and water. Stir until well blended. Place steel cutting blade into container. Add ice cream and 1½ cups orange juice. Process, using TOUCH-ON control, until smooth and creamy. Pour into tall glasses. Garnish with orange slice, if desired.

LEMON DELIGHT   Yield: Serves 6 to 8

A tart and pretty dessert that can be made well in advance.

1 (3-ounce) package lemon gelatin
1 cup boiling water
½ cup granulated sugar
1 tablespoon lemon juice

1 teaspoon grated lemon rind
5 (2" x 2") graham cracker squares
1 (13-ounce) can evaporated milk, chilled
Maraschino cherries

In a small bowl, dissolve lemon gelatin in boiling water. Add sugar, lemon juice, and lemon rind and stir until blended. Chill until mixture is partially set. While gelatin is cooling, place steel cutting blade into container. Add graham crackers. Process until crumbs are formed. Empty onto waxed paper. Place steel cutting blade into container. Add partially set gelatin. Process, while slowly pouring evaporated milk through feed tube. Continue processing until mixture is thoroughly combined. Pour into an ungreased 8" x 8" x 2" pan. Sprinkle graham cracker crumbs over top of mixture and decorate with maraschino cherries. Chill for several hours. Cut into squares and serve.

PISTACHIO-PINEAPPLE DESSERT   Yield: Serves 10 to 12

This is a creamy, summertime dessert.

1 baked 9" x 9" x 2" graham
  cracker crust (see page 105)
1 (3¾-ounce) package pistachio
  instant pudding
1¾ cups milk

1 cup frozen, whipped topping
1 (20-ounce) can crushed pineapple,
  drained
2 cups miniature marshmallows

Place steel cutting blade into container. Add instant pudding and milk. Process until well blended. Add frozen topping. Process, using TOUCH-ON control, until blended. Add pineapple and marshmallows. Process, using TOUCH-ON control, until just blended. Pour over prepared crust. Refrigerate at least 1 hour before serving.

STRAWBERRY SHORTCAKE   Yield: Serves 6 to 8

A joyful celebration of the strawberry season.

1 quart fresh strawberries, hulled
1⅓ cups granulated sugar, divided
2 cups sifted all-purpose flour
2½ teaspoons baking powder

½ teaspoon salt
¾ cup milk
¼ cup butter or margarine, melted
Whipped topping or whipped cream (optional)

Place slicing disc into container. Slice strawberries. Empty strawberries into a large bowl. Stir in 1 cup sugar. Refrigerate for several hours. Preheat oven to 400°F. Grease a 9" x 9" x 2" baking pan. Place steel cutting blade into container. Sift flour, ⅓ cup sugar, baking powder, and salt into the container. Add milk and butter. Process until mixture is just blended. DO NOT OVERPROCESS. Press mixture into bottom of prepared pan. Bake for 15 to 20 minutes. Split shortcake while warm. Fill and top with strawberries. Serve with whipped topping or whipped cream, if desired.

PARTY MINTS   Yield: 5 dozen

1 (3-ounce) package cream cheese
1 pound confectioners sugar, divided
1 tablespoon milk

2 drops mint extract
Food coloring

Place steel cutting blade into container. Add cream cheese. Process until smooth. Add half of confectioners sugar. Process until smooth. Repeat with remaining half. Slowly add remaining ingredients through feed tube. Continue processing until mixture is well blended. Pour into a glass bowl. Cover and chill for several hours. Roll into 1" balls and place onto waxed paper. Flatten balls with the tines of a fork or a flat, decorative object. Serve chilled.

PEANUT BUTTER CANDY   Yield: 36 pieces

½ cup salted cocktail-style peanuts
1 egg
2½ cups confectioners sugar, divided
½ teaspoon vanilla extract

2 tablespoons butter or margarine, softened
½ cup creamy peanut butter
1 teaspoon milk

Place steel cutting blade into container. Add peanuts and coarsely chop. Empty onto waxed paper. Place steel cutting blade into container. Add egg, 1 cup confectioners sugar, vanilla extract, butter, and peanut butter. Process to blend all ingredients. Remove cover and add remaining confectioners sugar. While processing all ingredients, pour milk down feed tube. Process until ingredients form a ball. Shape into 1" balls and roll in chopped peanuts. Place on waxed paper and refrigerate for 2 to 4 hours.

NUTTY FUDGE SQUARES   Yield: 64 squares

1 cup shelled walnuts, divided
1¼ cups confectioners sugar
3 tablespoons cocoa
Dash of salt
¼ cup butter or margarine, melted

¼ cup milk
½ teaspoon vanilla extract
1½ cups quick-cooking rolled oats
½ cup grated coconut

Place steel cutting blade into container. Coarsely chop walnuts. Empty onto waxed paper. Place steel cutting blade into container. Add confectioners sugar, cocoa, and salt. Process until well blended. Add butter, milk, and vanilla extract. Process until well blended, about 10 seconds. Remove cover and scrape down container sides. Add oats, coconut, and ½ cup chopped walnuts. Process, using TOUCH-ON control, only until blended. Turn into an ungreased 8" x 8" x 2" baking pan. Press into place. Top with remaining ½ cup chopped walnuts. Chill until firm, about 1 hour. Cut into 1" x 1" squares and serve.

CHOCOLATE SODA   Yield: Serves 1

2 to 3 scoops vanilla ice cream, divided
2 tablespoons chocolate syrup

2 tablespoons milk
Lemon-lime soda

Place steel cutting blade into container. Add 2 scoops ice cream, chocolate syrup, and milk. Process using TOUCH-ON control, until smooth and well blended. Empty into a tall glass and fill with soda. Add another scoop of ice cream, if desired.

THE PIZZA PARLOR

Chapter Nine

Homemade pizza, served right in your own parlor, can be yours with a little help from your food processor. You'll find recipes in this chapter for crusts and fillings. Find your favorite or make up your own.

DEEP-DISH PIZZA CRUST   Yield: 1 12" pizza crust

2¼ cups sifted all-purpose flour
1 package active dry yeast
1 teaspoon granulated sugar
1 teaspoon salt

½ cup warm water (120° to 130°F)
1 egg, slightly beaten
¼ cup vegetable oil
1 tablespoon yellow cornmeal

Preheat oven to 375°F. Place steel cutting blade into container. Add flour. Sprinkle yeast, sugar, and salt over flour. Pour water over ingredients. Let rest 2 minutes. Add egg and oil. Process just until dough ball is formed, adding extra flour if necessary. Dough should be slightly sticky. Place in lightly greased bowl; cover with towel. Set in warm place. Allow to rise for ½ hour. Lightly grease a 12" round pizza pan and sprinkle with cornmeal. Press dough into pan. Spread crust with desired sauce and toppings. Bake for 20 to 30 minutes. Slice and serve immediately.

WHOLE WHEAT PIZZA CRUST   Yield: 1 12" crust

1 tablespoon yellow cornmeal
1 package active dry yeast
¾ cup water (105° to 115°F)
2 teaspoons granulated sugar

½ teaspoon salt
2 tablespoons vegetable oil
1½ cups sifted all-purpose flour
1 cup whole wheat flour

Preheat oven to 400°F. Grease a 12" round pizza pan. Sprinkle with cornmeal to coat pan. Dissolve yeast in warm water. Place steel cutting blade into container. Pour dissolved yeast into container. Add sugar, salt, oil, and all-purpose flour. Process until well blended, about 10 to 15 seconds. Allow mixture to rise for 30 minutes in the processor container. Add whole wheat flour. Process only until dough ball forms. Remove dough from container onto floured surface. Knead for 1 minute. Roll into a 13" circle. Place on prepared pizza pan. Form a ridge around the edge with the dough. Spread crust with desired sauce and toppings. Bake for 20 minutes, or until crust is lightly browned. Slice and serve immediately.

OLD-FASHIONED PIZZA CRUST   Yield: 2 12" crusts

2 cups + 1 tablespoon flour
2 teaspoons baking powder
½ teaspoon salt

⅔ cup milk
¼ cup salad oil

Preheat oven to 425°F. Place steel cutting blade into container. Add flour, baking powder, and salt. While processor is running, add milk, then oil, through feed tube. Process until a dough ball is formed. Divide dough into two halves. On a lightly floured board, roll each half into a 13" circle.

   Place on a 12" pizza pan or cookie sheet, forming a ½" edge all around. Bake for 5 minutes. Spread crust with desired sauce and toppings. Bake for 15 to 25 minutes. Slice and serve immediately.

FRENCH BREAD LOAF PIZZA   Yield: Serves 4

1 loaf French Bread, baked
  (see page 86)
1 (15-ounce) can tomato sauce
½ pound ground beef, cooked
  and drained

½ pound fresh mushrooms
1 small green pepper, cored
8 ounces Mozzarella cheese
1 tablespoon oregano

Preheat oven to BROIL. Lightly grease a cookie sheet. Cut French Bread in half, lengthwise. Place bread halves onto prepared cookie sheet. Brush tomato sauce onto each half of bread and top with ground beef. Place slicing disc into container. Slice mushrooms and empty onto a sheet of waxed paper. Slice green pepper and empty onto a sheet of waxed paper. Position mushrooms and green pepper on top of the ground beef. Place shredding disc into container. Shred Mozzarella cheese. Top pizza with Mozzarella cheese and sprinkle with oregano. Broil for 5 to 10 minutes, or until cheese is bubbly. Cut into pieces and serve immediately.

MEXICAN TACO PIZZA   Yield: Serves 4 to 6

1 unbaked 12" deep-dish pizza crust
  (see page 145)
¼ pound ground beef
8 ounces Cheddar cheese
2 cups corn chips
1 (15½-ounce) can red kidney beans
1 (8-ounce) can tomato sauce

1 small tomato, quartered
1 small onion, peeled and quartered
1 clove garlic, peeled
½ teaspoon chili powder
½ teaspoon salt
¼ head of lettuce, washed, drained,
  and cut into wedges

Preheat oven to 400°F. Brown ground beef in frypan. Drain and set aside. Place shredding disc into container. Shred cheese. Empty onto a sheet of waxed paper. Place steel cutting blade into container. Coarsely crush corn chips. Empty onto a sheet of waxed paper. Add kidney beans, tomato sauce, tomato, onion, garlic, chili powder, and salt to the container. Process until smooth. Pour over prepared pizza crust. Spread to within ½" of crust's edge. Top with ground beef. Bake 10 minutes. Remove from oven. Sprinkle with crushed corn chips and cheese. Bake an additional 10 to 15 minutes, or until cheese is lightly browned. Meanwhile, place slicing disc into container. Slice lettuce. Sprinkle lettuce over baked pizza. Serve immediately.

SUNDAY BRUNCH PIZZA   Yield: Serves 4 to 6

1 (6-ounce) can tomato paste
1 unbaked 12″ whole wheat pizza crust
  (see page 145)
½ teaspoon oregano
¼ pound fresh mushrooms
1 small green pepper, cored

8 ounces Mozzarella cheese
2 tablespoons butter or margarine
½ pound cooked bacon slices (crisp)
3 sprigs parsley
4 eggs

Preheat oven to 400°F. Spread tomato paste over prepared crust to within ½″ of edges. Sprinkle with oregano. Place slicing disc into container. Slice mushrooms and green pepper. Spread over pizza. Place shredding disc into container. Shred cheese. Sprinkle half of the shredded cheese over pizza. Bake pizza for 15 to 20 minutes, or until cheese is lightly browned. Meanwhile, empty remaining cheese onto a sheet of waxed paper. In a frypan, melt butter. Place steel cutting blade into container. Add bacon and parsley. Process until coarsely chopped. Empty onto a sheet of waxed paper. Place steel cutting blade into container. Add eggs and process until foamy. Pour into frypan. Scramble eggs over low heat. Remove pizza from oven. Cover with scrambled eggs. Top with bacon and parsley mixture, then remaining cheese. Return to oven, until cheese is melted. Slice and serve immediately.

VEGETARIAN PIZZA   Yield: Serves 4 to 6

1 (6-ounce) can tomato paste
1 medium tomato, quartered
1 small onion, peeled and
  quartered
¼ cup water
½ teaspoon oregano
½ teaspoon salt

Dash of pepper
1 unbaked 12″ round, deep-dish pizza crust
  (see page 145)
12 ounces Mozzarella cheese
1 small zucchini
1 small green pepper, cored
½ pound mushrooms

Preheat oven to 400°F. Place steel cutting blade into container. Add tomato paste, tomato, onion, water, oregano, salt, and pepper. Process until smooth. Pour sauce over prepared pizza crust. Spread within ½″ of edge. Place shredding disc into container. Shred cheese. Empty onto a sheet of waxed paper. Place slicing disc into container. Slice zucchini, green pepper, and mushrooms. Sprinkle over tomato sauce. Top with shredded cheese. Bake for 20 to 25 minutes, or until cheese is lightly browned. Slice and serve immediately.

Variation: Add chopped olives or sliced onions to pizza.

CHEESY PIZZA Yield: Serves 4 to 6

1 recipe unbaked Old-Fashioned Pizza
  Crust (see page 145)
1 (15-ounce) can tomato sauce
1 to 2 ounces Romano cheese,
  cut into 1" cubes

3 to 4 ounces Parmesan cheese,
  cut into 1" cubes
1 pound Mozzarella cheese
1 tablespoon oregano

Preheat oven to 425°F. Spread sauce over crust to within ½" of edge. Place steel cutting blade into container. Process Romano cheese until finely grated. Empty onto a sheet of waxed paper. Place steel cutting blade into container. Process Parmesan cheese until finely grated. Empty onto a sheet of waxed paper. Place shredding disc into container. Shred Mozzarella cheese. Sprinkle Romano cheese, Parmesan cheese, Mozzarella cheese, and oregano over crust and sauce. Bake 15 to 25 minutes. Slice and serve immediately.

Serving Suggestion: Cheesy Pizza can be baked on the Deep-Dish Pizza Crust by cutting the tomato sauce and oregano in half. Use the same amount of cheeses. Bake at 375°F for 20 to 30 minutes.

VARIETY PIZZA   Yield: Serves 4 to 6

CHOOSE ONE OF THESE CRUSTS:

Deep-Dish Pizza Crust (see page 145)   Old-Fashioned Pizza Crust (see page 145)
Whole Wheat Pizza Crust (see page 145)

BASIC INGREDIENTS:

7½ to 15 ounces tomato sauce
1 to 2 ounces Romano cheese,
   cut into 1" cubes

3 to 4 ounces Parmesan cheese,
   cut into 1" cubes
1 pound Mozzarella cheese
½ to 1 tablespoon oregano

CHOOSE ANY COMBINATION OF THE FOLLOWING INGREDIENTS:

½ pound mushrooms
1 medium green pepper,
   cored and halved
1 small onion, peeled
2 to 3 scallions
½ stick Pepperoni

3 frankfurters
10 to 20 stuffed green olives
   or black ripe olives
½ pound cooked ground beef, drained
½ pound pork sausage, browned and drained

Preheat oven according to crust recipe directions. Prepare crust. Spread sauce over crust to within ½" of edge. Place steel cutting blade into container. Process Romano cheese until finely grated. Empty onto a sheet of waxed paper. Place steel cutting blade into container. Process Parmesan cheese until finely grated. Empty onto a sheet of waxed paper. Place shredding disc into container. Shred Mozzarella cheese. Empty onto a sheet of waxed paper. Place slicing disc into container. Choose your combination of ingredients. Slice separately, mushrooms, green pepper, onion, scallions, Pepperoni, frankfurters, and/or olives. Place ingredients over sauce. Top pizza with Romano cheese, Parmesan cheese, Mozzarella cheese, and oregano. Bake according to crust recipe directions. Slice and serve immediately.

THE SAUCEPAN

Chapter Ten

Smooth and creamy, savory sauces are the well-known secret of gourmet cooking. The right sauce can make a simple dish elegant, and make a leftover taste delicious. The food processor is just what you need to shred the cheese for Swiss Cheese Sauce, chop the vegetables for Sauce Verte, and mix Sweet-Sour Basting Sauce. There are many more, and you can create your own by simply changing an ingredient. It's the last touch, but never least important.

SWISS CHEESE SAUCE   Yield: About 2 cups

6 ounces Swiss cheese
2 tablespoons butter or margarine
2 tablespoons sifted all-purpose flour

2 cups milk
½ teaspoon salt
Dash of black pepper

Place shredding disc into container. Shred Swiss cheese. In a saucepan, melt butter. Blend in flour; gradually add milk. Cook until mixture boils, stirring constantly. Season with salt and pepper. Add shredded cheese. Stir until cheese is melted and sauce is thickened. Serve immediately.

Serving Suggestion: Combine 2 (7-ounce) cans tuna and Swiss cheese sauce in a 1-quart casserole. Top with buttered bread crumbs. Bake at 400°F for 30 minutes. Serve hot.

CHEESE SAUCE   Yield: 2½ cups

8 ounces American cheese
¼ cup butter or margarine

¼ cup sifted all-purpose flour
1 cup milk

Place shredding disc into container. Shred cheese. Empty onto a sheet of waxed **paper**. Melt butter in a saucepan over low heat. Add flour and stir until smooth. Gradually add milk, and continue stirring. Heat to boiling. Add shredded cheese and stir until cheese melts. Serve hot over cooked vegetables.

SAUCE VERTE   Yield: 2 cups

3 tablespoons salad oil
1 cup spinach leaves, torn into pieces
½ cup parsley sprigs

1 clove garlic, peeled
2 tablespoons chives
1¼ cups mayonnaise

Place steel cutting blade into container. Add oil, spinach, parsley, garlic, and chives. Process until finely chopped. Add mayonnaise. Process only until blended. Serve over hot or cold vegetables.

SWEET-SOUR BASTING SAUCE   Yield: 1 cup

1 (6-ounce) can frozen pineapple juice
   concentrate
½ cup wine vinegar
⅓ cup brown sugar
¼ green pepper, cut into 1" chunks
½ jar (2 ounces) pimiento

1 teaspoon soy sauce
½ teaspoon salt
½ clove garlic
Pineapple chunks (optional)
Green pepper strips (optional)

Place steel cutting blade into container. Add pineapple juice concentrate, wine vinegar, brown sugar, green pepper, pimiento, soy sauce, salt, and garlic. Process until thoroughly blended. Brush on pork or chicken while it broils, roasts, or barbecues. Garnish with pineapple chunks and green pepper strips before serving, if desired.

WESTERN BARBECUE SAUCE   Yield: 2½ cups

1 (14-ounce) bottle tomato ketchup
½ cup undiluted consommé
⅓ cup salad oil
¼ cup wine vinegar

1 tablespoon soy sauce
2 tablespoons brown sugar
½ teaspoon salt
⅛ teaspoon garlic powder

Place steel cutting blade into container. Add all ingredients. Process until well blended. Pour into saucepan and heat. Use as a barbecue sauce for chicken, steak, chops, or fish.

SPICY SAUCE   Yield: About 3 cups

2 (12-ounce) bottles chili sauce
2 tablespoons Worcestershire sauce
2 tablespoons sweet pickle relish

1 tablespoon brown sugar
¼ teaspoon garlic salt
¼ teaspoon onion salt

Place steel cutting blade into container. Add all ingredients. Process until well blended. Heat before serving.

Serving Suggestion: Pour over meatballs or frankfurters that have been cut into 1" pieces. Serve with toothpicks as an appetizer.

CREAMY CUCUMBER SAUCE   Yield: 1 cup

1 medium cucumber, seeded and cut
   into 1" chunks
1 cup sour cream
   or plain lowfat yogurt

1 teaspoon dill weed
2 teaspoons minced onion
Salt and pepper to taste

Place steel cutting blade into container. Add all ingredients and process for 5 seconds. Serve with fresh vegetables or baked fish.

LEMON PARSLEY SAUCE   Yield: ½ cup

1 lemon, peeled, quartered and seeded
1 medium onion, peeled and quartered

½ cup parsley sprigs
½ teaspoon salt

Place steel cutting blade into container. Add all ingredients. Process until finely chopped. Brush on fish while baking, broiling, or barbecuing.

QUICK HOLLANDAISE SAUCE   Yield: ¾ cup

1 egg
2 tablespoons lemon juice
¼ teaspoon salt

Pinch of cayenne pepper
½ cup butter or margarine, melted

Place steel cutting blade into container. Add egg, lemon juice, salt, and cayenne pepper. Process, while slowly pouring melted butter through feed tube. Continue processing until smooth. Pour into a small saucepan. Stir over low heat, only until thickened. Serve warm over vegetables.

FRUIT SAUCE   Yield: 1¼ cups

¼ cup orange marmalade
1 teaspoon prepared mustard

¾ cup currant jelly
¼ cup boiling water

Place steel cutting blade into container. Add marmalade, mustard, and jelly. Process, while slowly pouring water down feed tube. Continue processing until thoroughly blended. Use to baste ham.

MEAT SAUCE   Yield: 7 to 8 cups

Two cups of beef cubes will be chopped fine in a twinkling.

1 large onion, peeled and quartered
1 clove garlic, peeled
2 tablespoons vegetable oil
1½ pounds ground beef,
   browned and drained
1 (28-ounce) can Italian tomatoes
1 (10-ounce) can Italian tomatoes
1 (8-ounce) can tomato sauce

1 (6-ounce) can tomato paste
¼ cup red wine
2 tablespoons Worcestershire sauce
2 teaspoons salt
1 teaspoon seasoned salt
1 teaspoon granulated sugar
1 tablespoon basil
2 tablespoons oregano

Place steel cutting blade into container. Add onion and garlic. Process until finely chopped. Empty into a large saucepan or Dutch oven with oil. Cook until tender. Add cooked ground beef. Place steel cutting blade into container. Add tomatoes. Process using TOUCH-ON control, about 2 times. Empty into saucepan with onion mixture. Place steel cutting blade into container. Add tomato sauce, tomato paste, wine, Worcestershire sauce, salt, seasoned salt, granulated sugar, basil, and oregano. Process, using TOUCH-ON control, only once. Empty into saucepan with tomato mixture. Stir. Cover and simmer 1½ hours, stirring occasionally. Serve hot over spaghetti.

THE
INDEX